Bateman, Charles.
Exciting easy classics
for piano /
c1996.
33305205514023
ca   04/13/04

Exciting Easy Classics

For Piano

Arranged by Charles Bateman

THE
CREATIVE
CONCEPTS
LIBRARY

BOOK ONE

D1737352

Catalog #07-2053

ISBN# 1-56922-161-8

©1996 CREATIVE CONCEPTS PUBLISHING CORPORATION
All Rights Reserved

*No part of this book may be reproduced or transmitted in any form
or by any means, electronic or mechanical without permission in writing
from the publisher: Creative Concepts Publishing Corp.*

Cover Painting by Mary Woodin - London, England

EXCLUSIVELY DISTRIBUTED BY

CREATIVE CON~~CEPTS~~ **·LEONARD**®
P U B L I S H~~ING~~ ~~COR~~PORATION

SANTA CLARA COUNTY LIBRARY

3 3305 20551 4023

www.halleonard.com

CONTENTS

CONTENTS

ADAGIETTO
(from Symphony No. 5)

Gustav Mahler

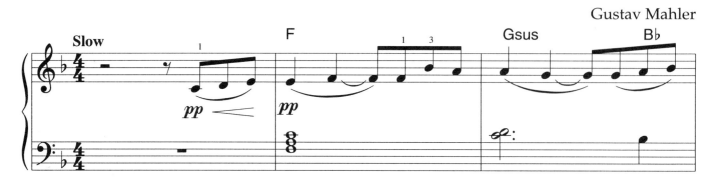

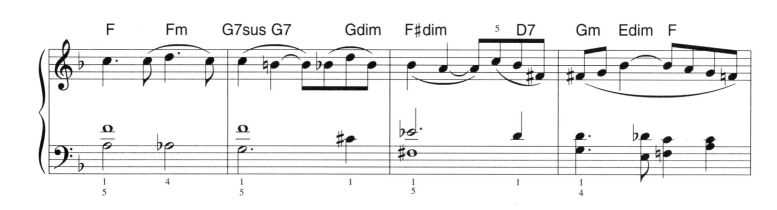

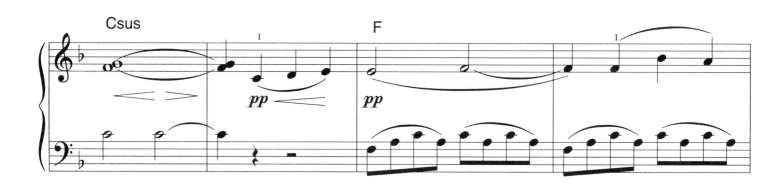

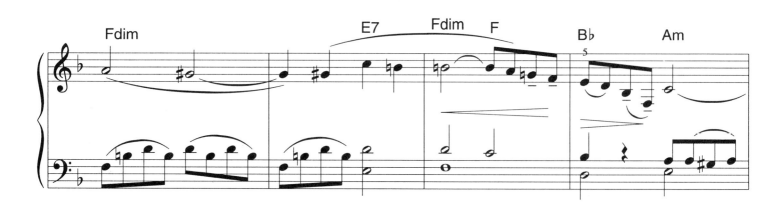

© 1996 Creative Concepts Publishing Corporation
All Rights Reserved

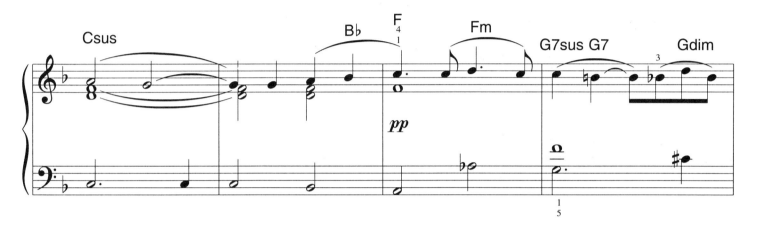

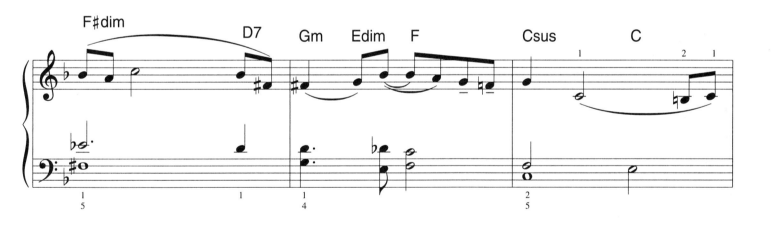

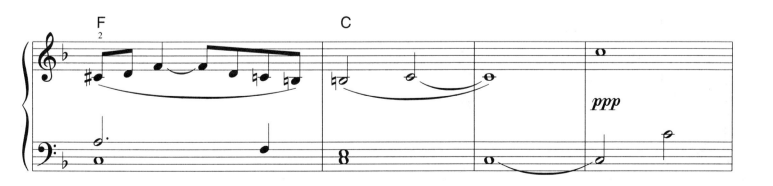

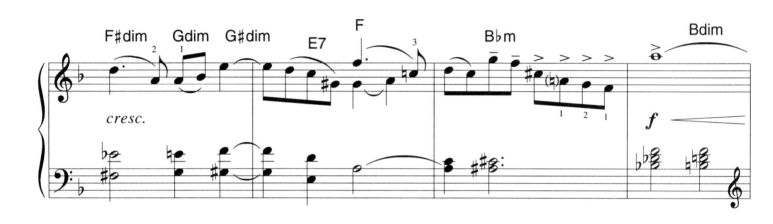

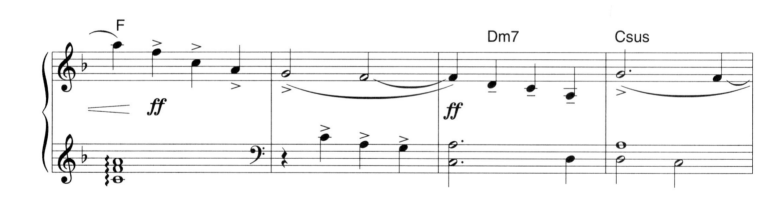

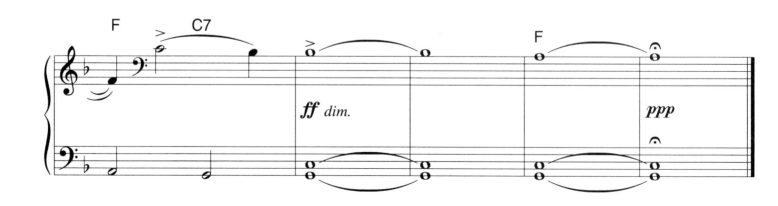

ANDANTE
(from Symphony No. 7)

Ludwig van Beethoven

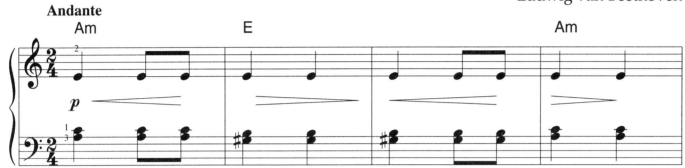

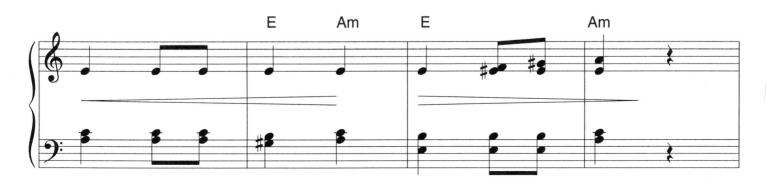

© 1996 Creative Concepts Publishing Corporation
All Rights Reserved

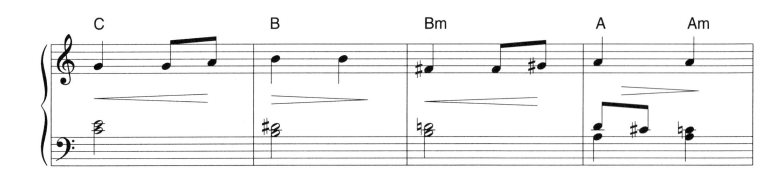

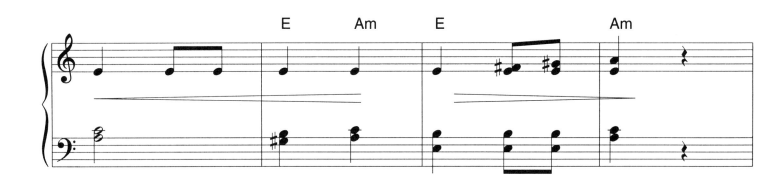

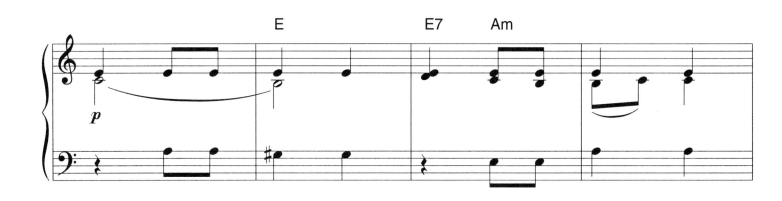

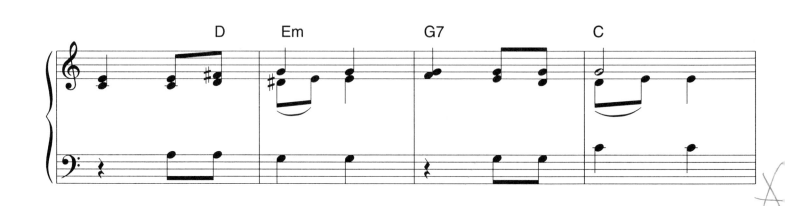

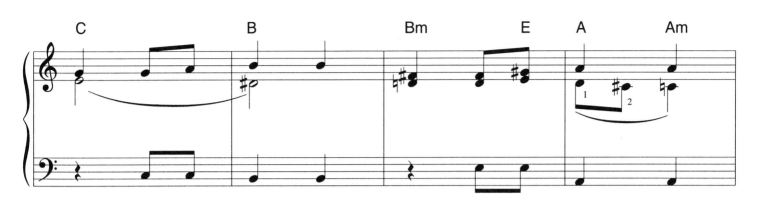

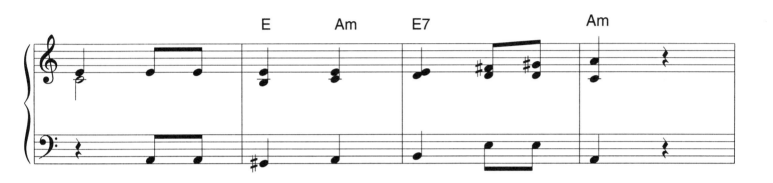

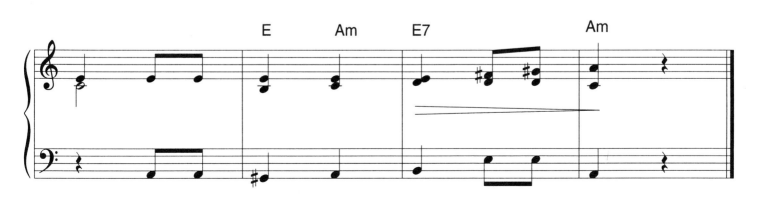

ARIOSO

Johann Sebastian Bach

Largo

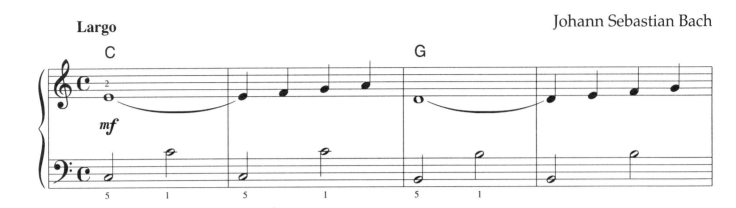

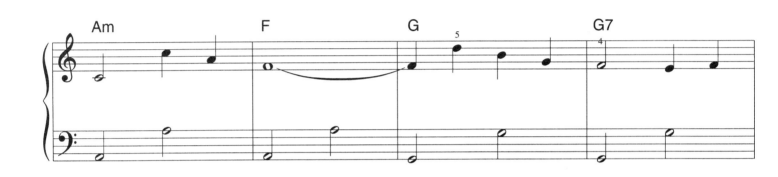

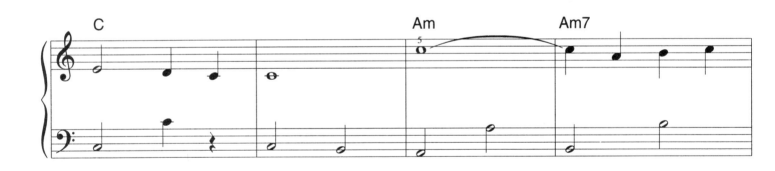

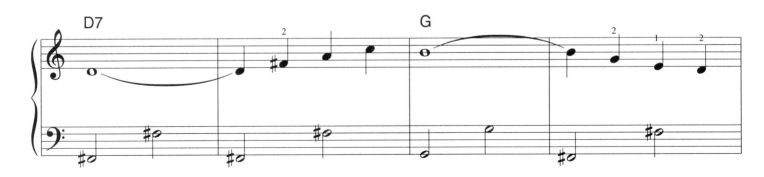

© 1996 Creative Concepts Publishing Corporation
All Rights Reserved

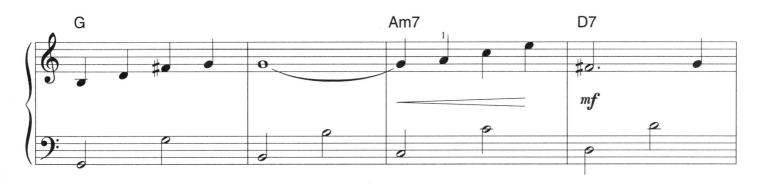

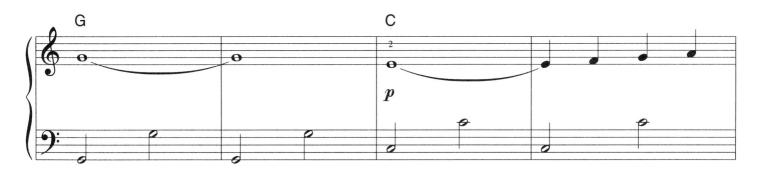

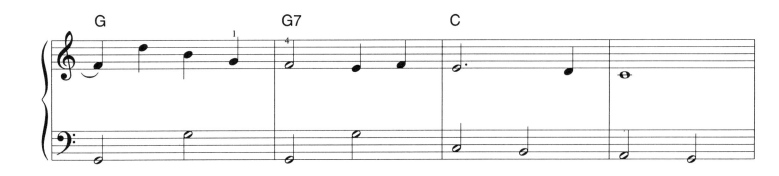

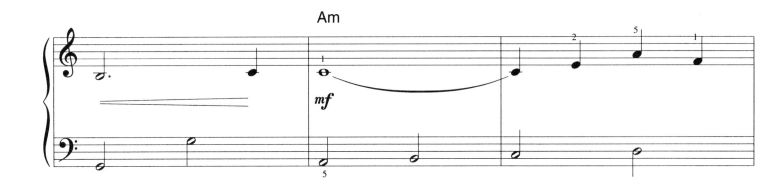

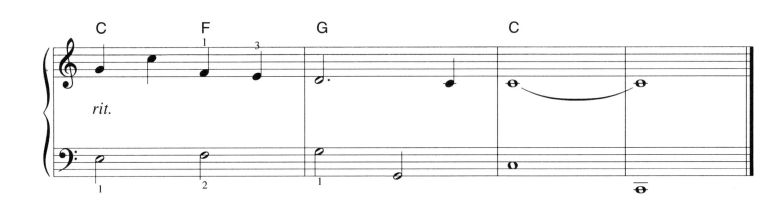

CAN CAN
(from "Orpheus")

Jacques Offenbach

© 1996 Creative Concepts Publishing Corporation
All Rights Reserved

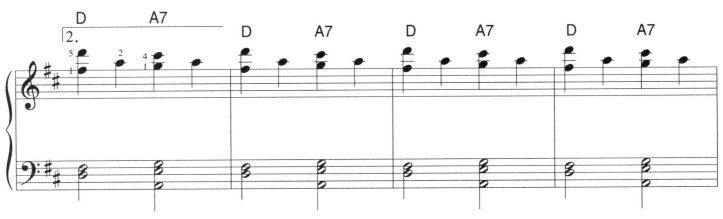

AUTUMN
(from "The Four Seasons")

Antonio Vivaldi

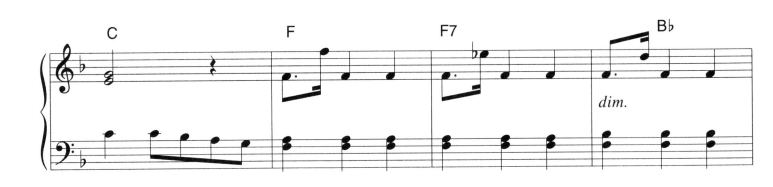

© 1996 Creative Concepts Publishing Corporation
All Rights Reserved

Theme from
CONCERTO IN C MAJOR

Antonio Vivaldi

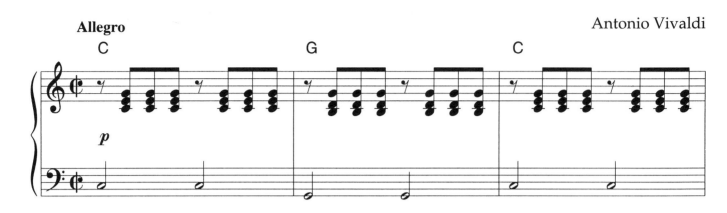

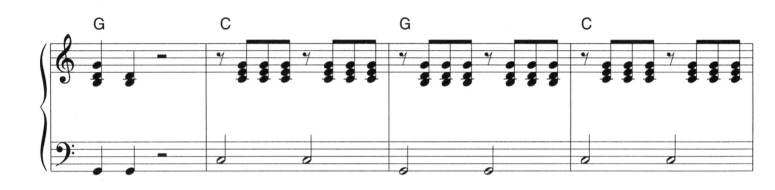

© 1996 Creative Concepts Publishing Corporation
All Rights Reserved

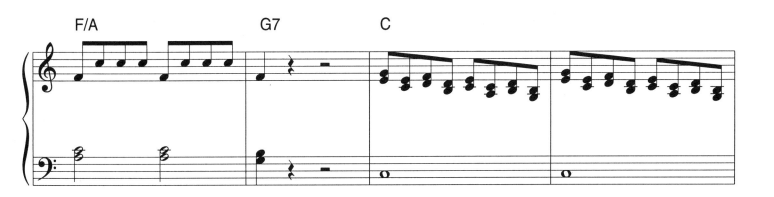

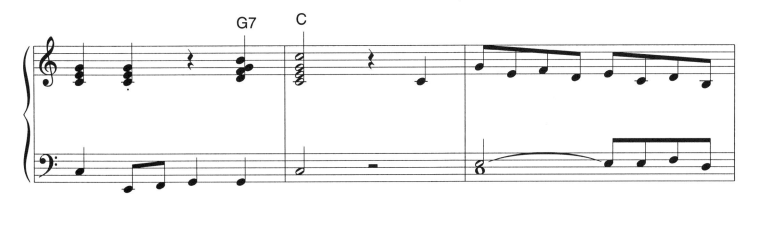

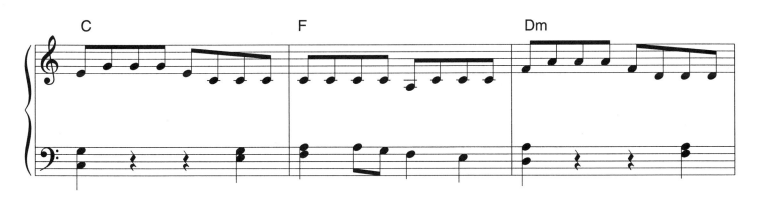

CONCERTO IN F
(SECOND MOVEMENT)

Wolfgang Amadeus Mozart

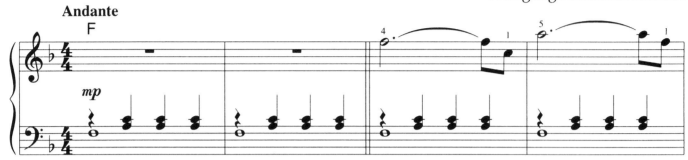

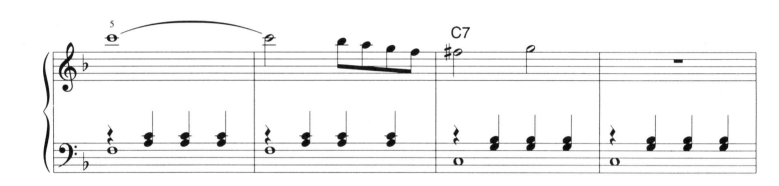

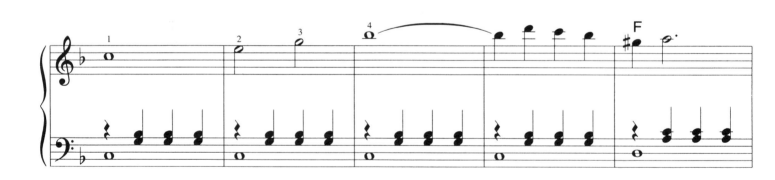

© 1996 Creative Concepts Publishing Corporation
All Rights Reserved

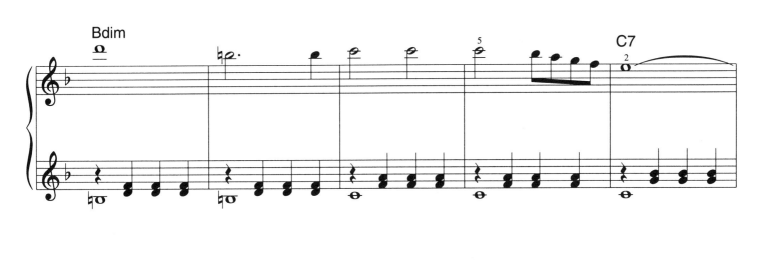

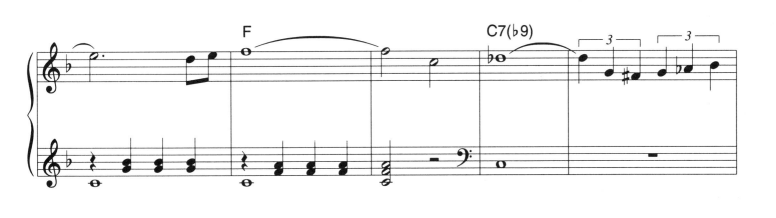

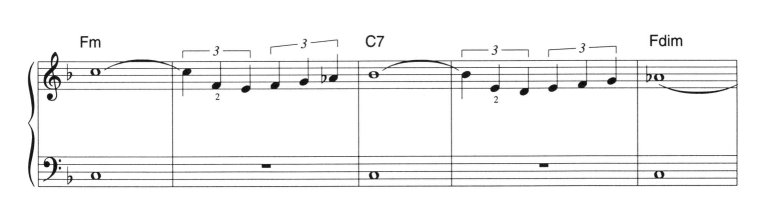

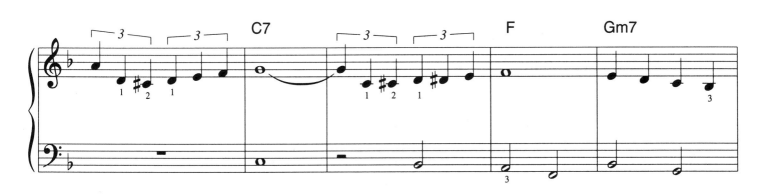

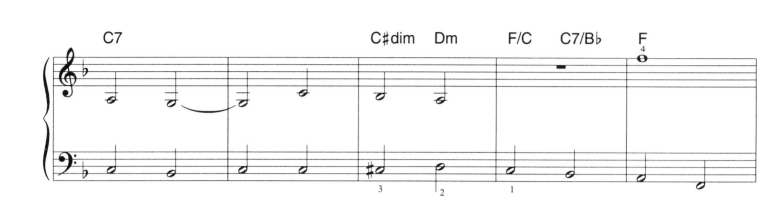

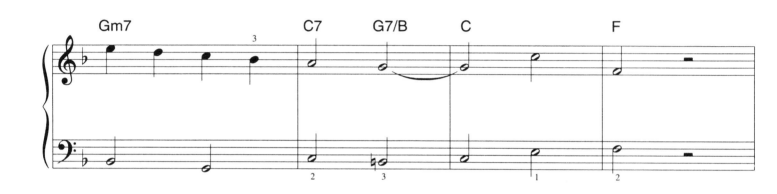

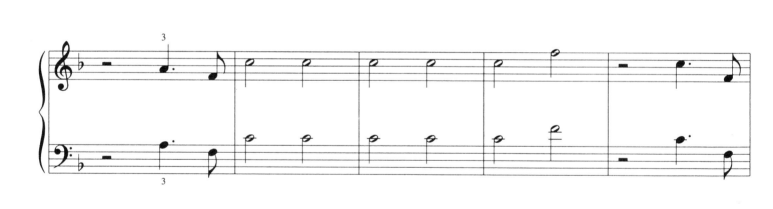

DANCE MACABRE

Camille Saint-Saëns

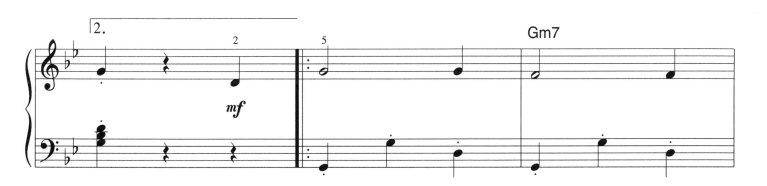

© 1996 Creative Concepts Publishing Corporation
All Rights Reserved

DANCE OF THE REED FLUTES
(from "The Nut Cracker Suite")

Pyotr Ilich Tchaikovsky

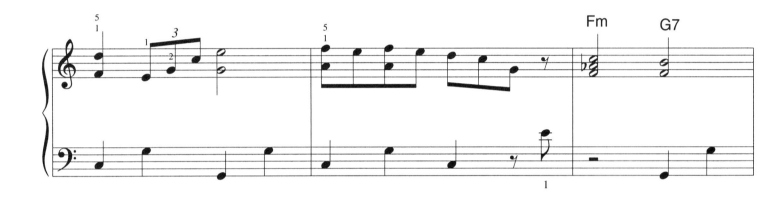

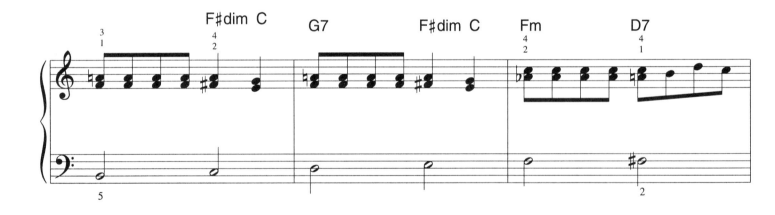

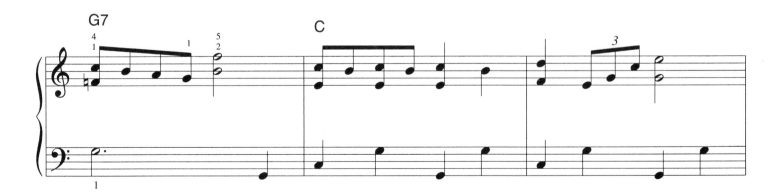

© 1996 Creative Concepts Publishing Corporation
All Rights Reserved

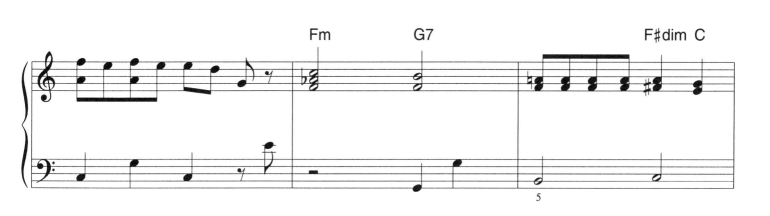

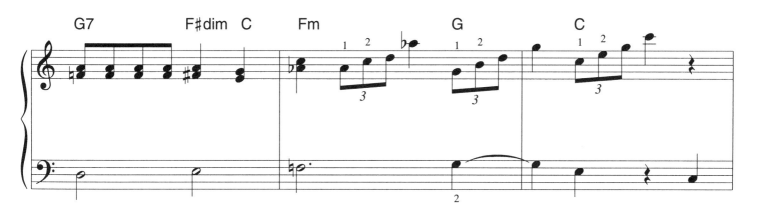

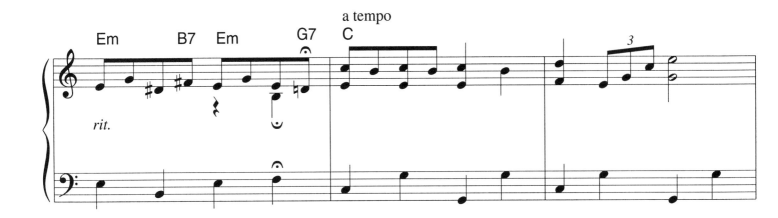

1ST MOVEMENT THEME
(FROM EINE KLEINE NACHTMUSIK)

Wolfgang Amadeus Mozart

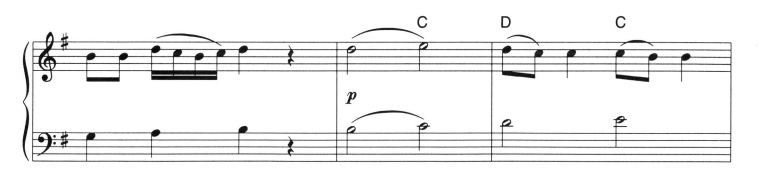

© 1996 Creative Concepts Publishing Corporation
All Rights Reserved

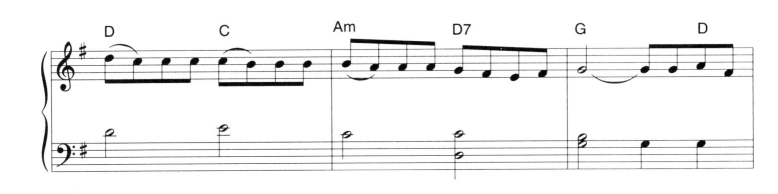

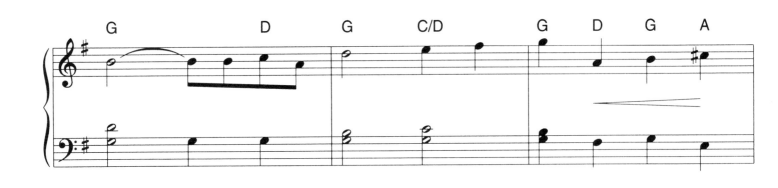

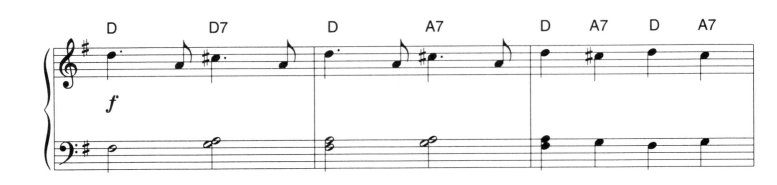

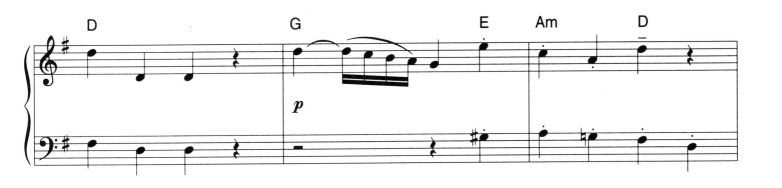

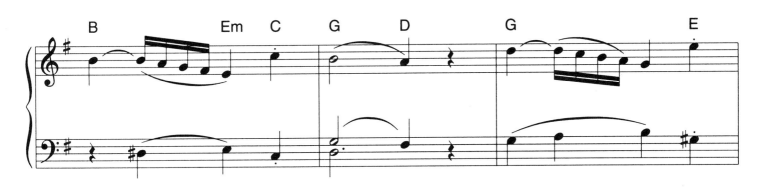

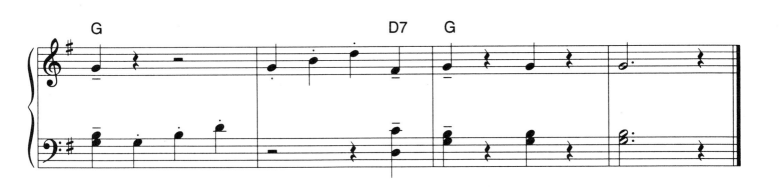

CHI BEL SOGNO DI DORETTA
(from "La Rondine")

Giacomo Puccini

Copyright © 1992 by HAL LEONARD CORPORATION
International Copyright Secured   All Rights Reserved

EMPEROR WALTZ

Johann Strauss

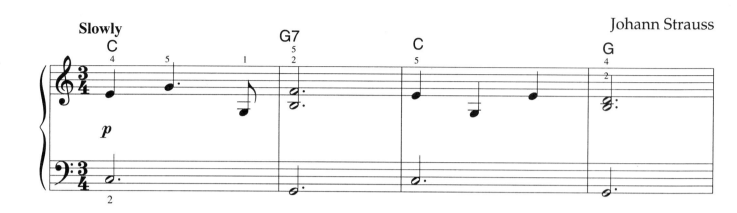

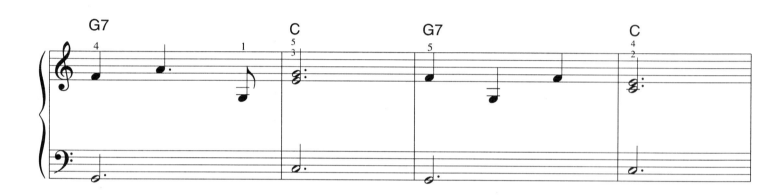

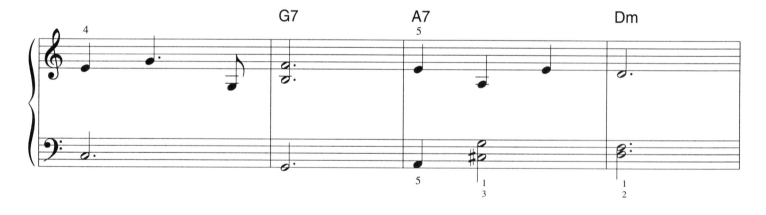

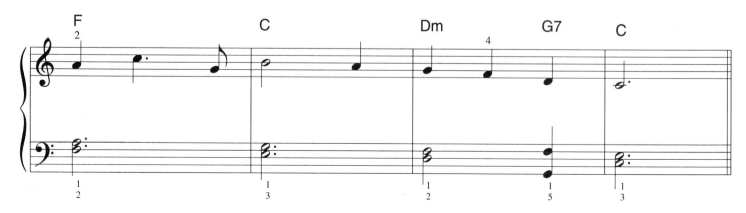

© 1996 Creative Concepts Publishing Corporation
All Rights Reserved

ENTRÉE
(from "Giselle")

Adolphe Adam

© 1996 Creative Concepts Publishing Corporation
All Rights Reserved

EROICA
(Theme from Symphony No. 3 in E♭)

Ludwig van Beethoven

Bright tempo

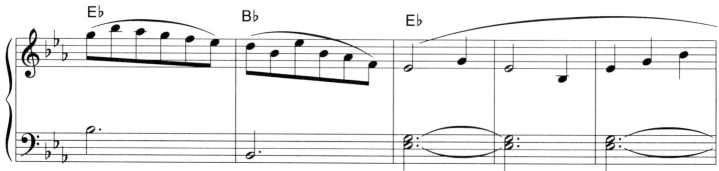

© 1996 Creative Concepts Publishing Corporation
All Rights Reserved

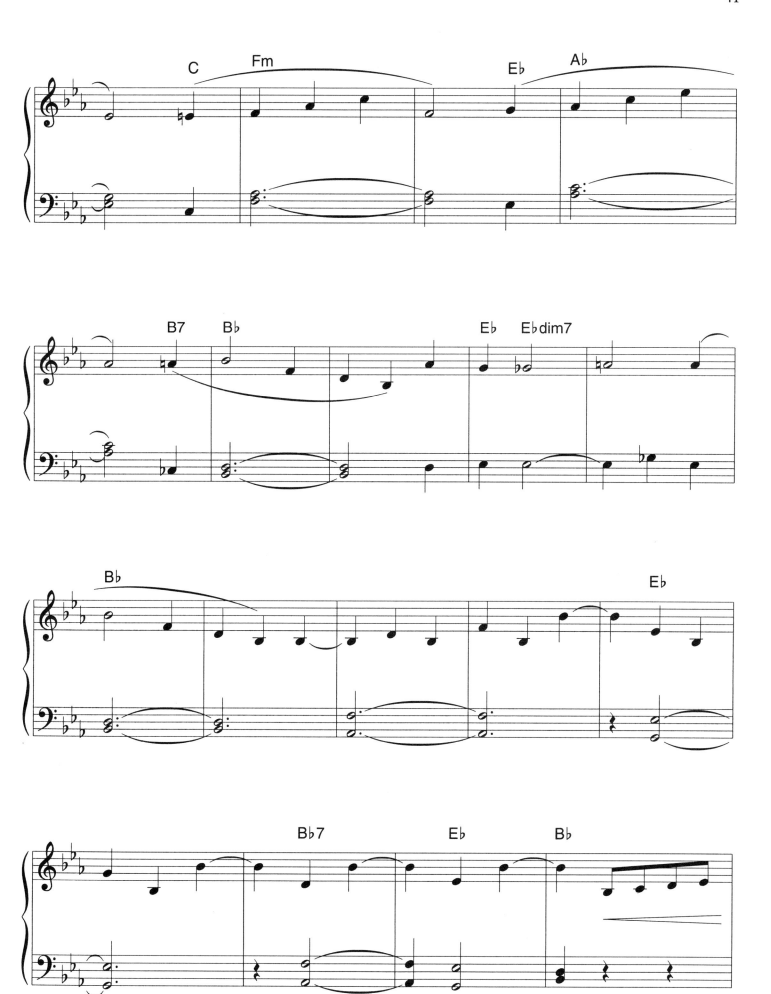

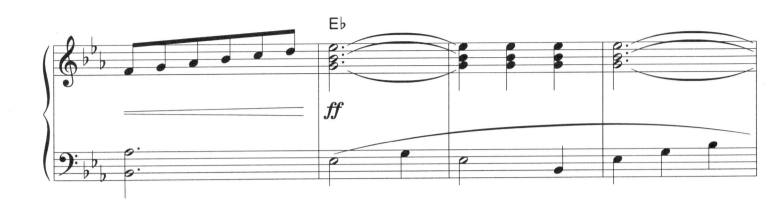

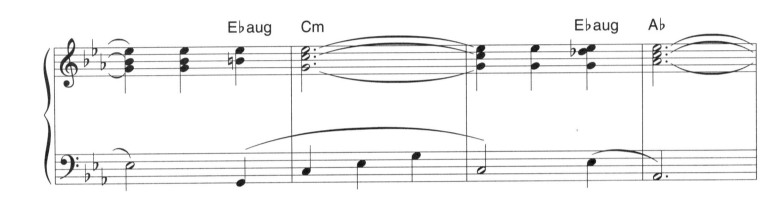

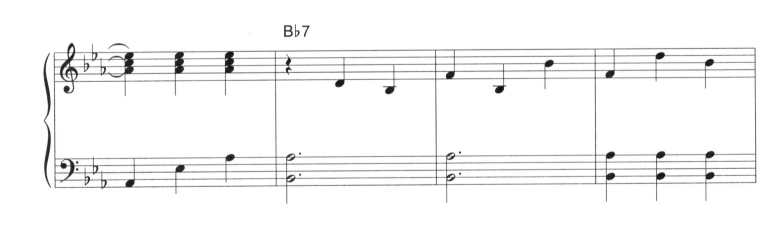

FARANDOLE
(from "L'Arlésienne")

Georges Bizet

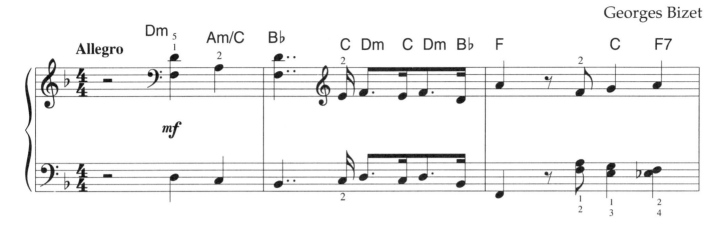

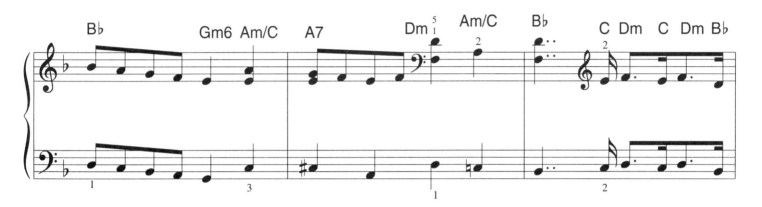

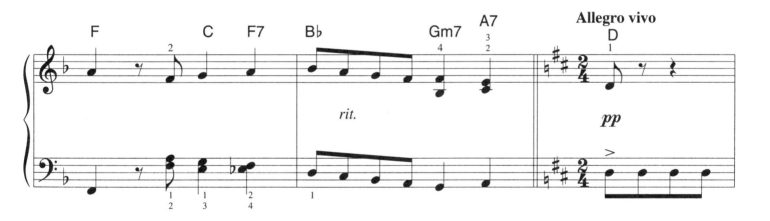

© 1996 Creative Concepts Publishing Corporation
All Rights Reserved

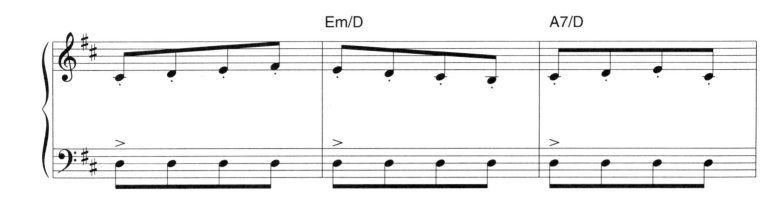

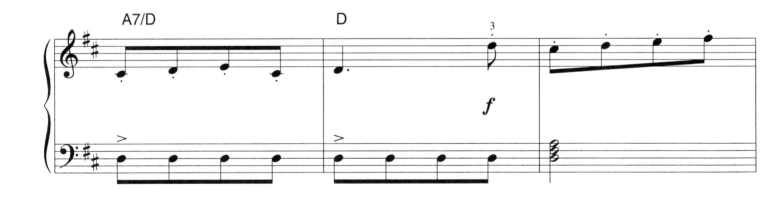

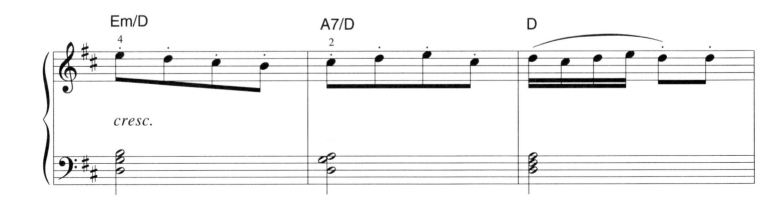

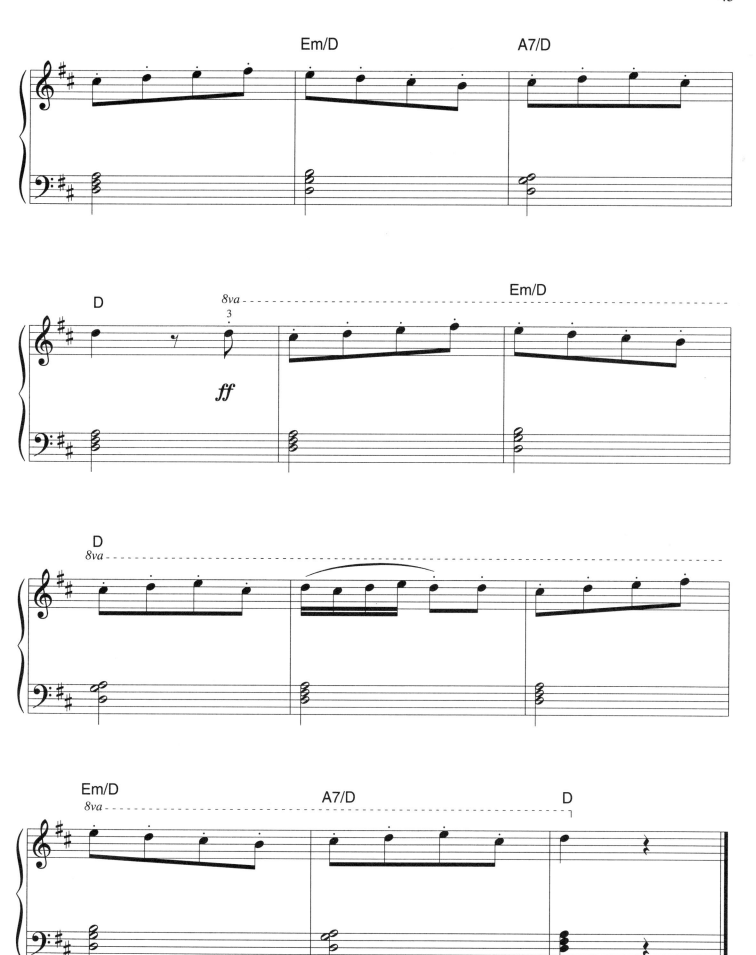

ETUDE IN E
(Opus 10, No. 3)

Frederic Chopin

Lento ma non troppo

© 1996 Creative Concepts Publishing Corporation
All Rights Reserved

EVENING STAR

Richard Wagner

© 1996 Creative Concepts Publishing Corporation
All Rights Reserved

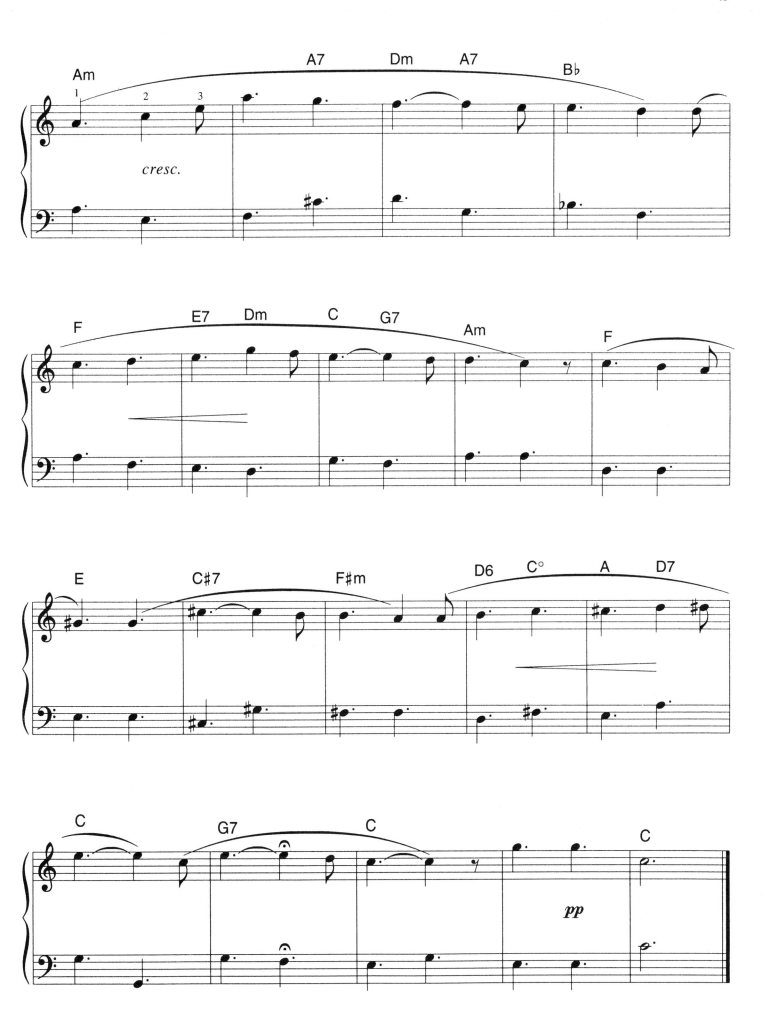

Theme from the
FIFTH SYMPHONY

Pyotr Ilyich Tchaikovsky

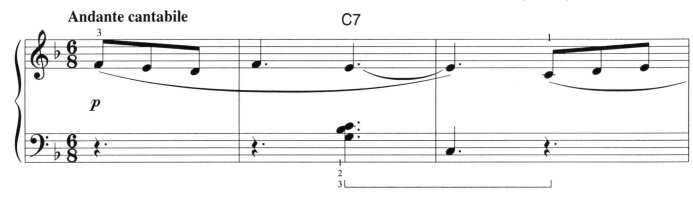

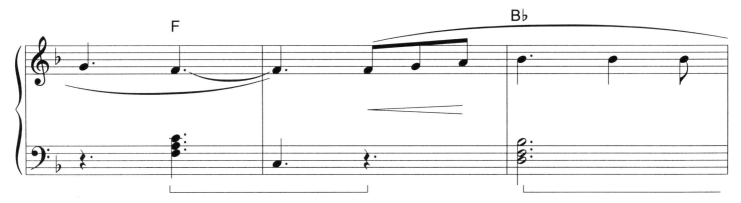

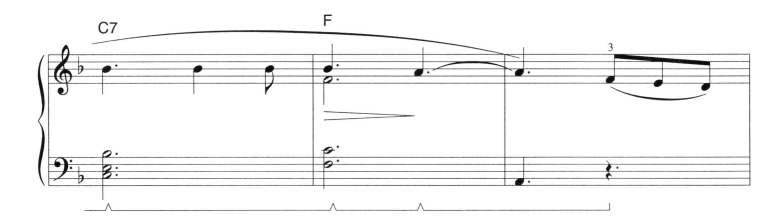

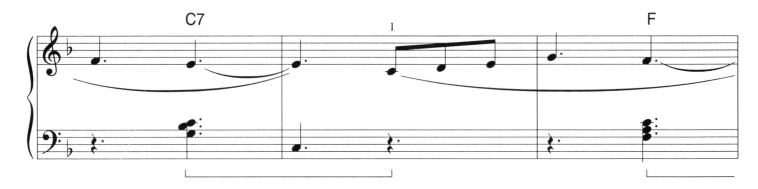

© 1996 Creative Concepts Publishing Corporation
All Rights Reserved

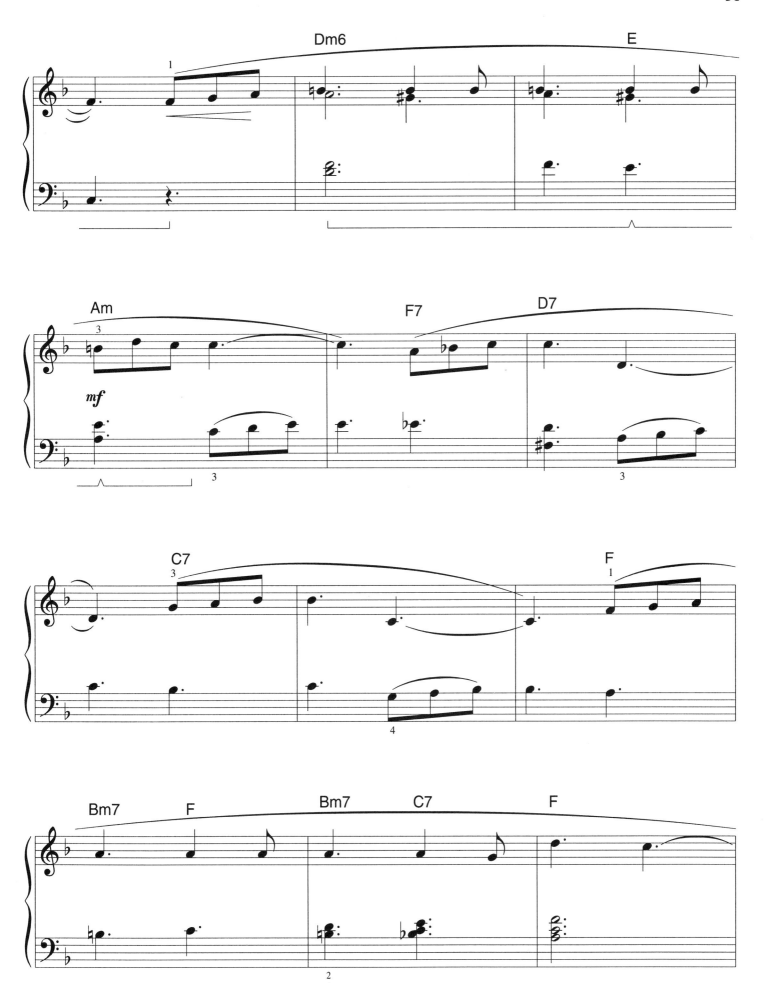

GALOP
(from "Orphée aux enfers")

Jacques Offenbach

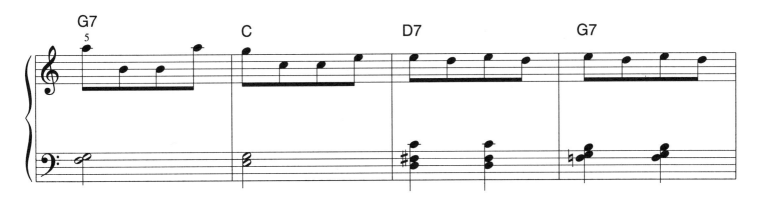

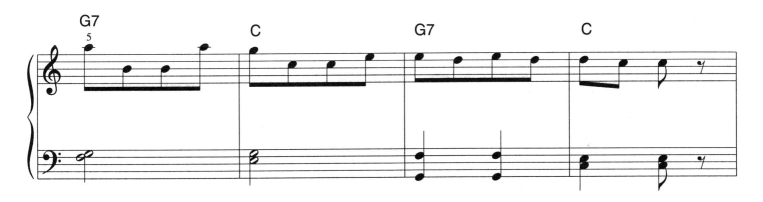

© 1996 Creative Concepts Publishing Corporation
All Rights Reserved

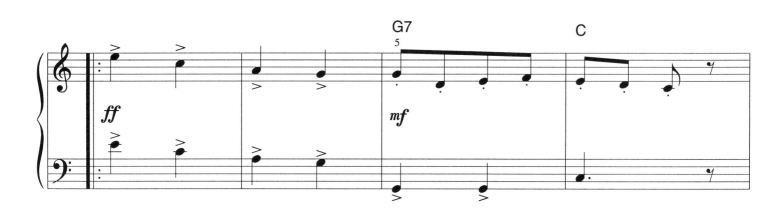

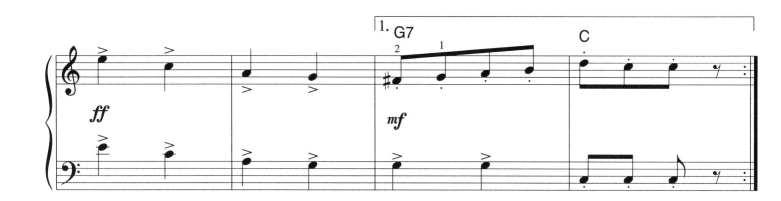

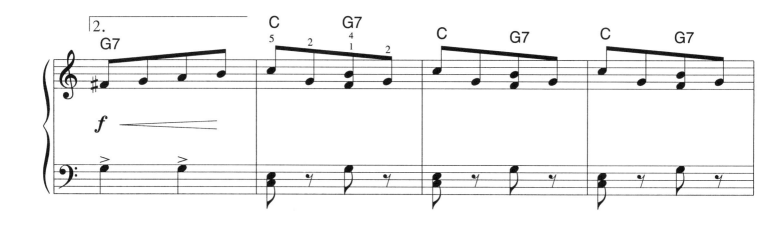

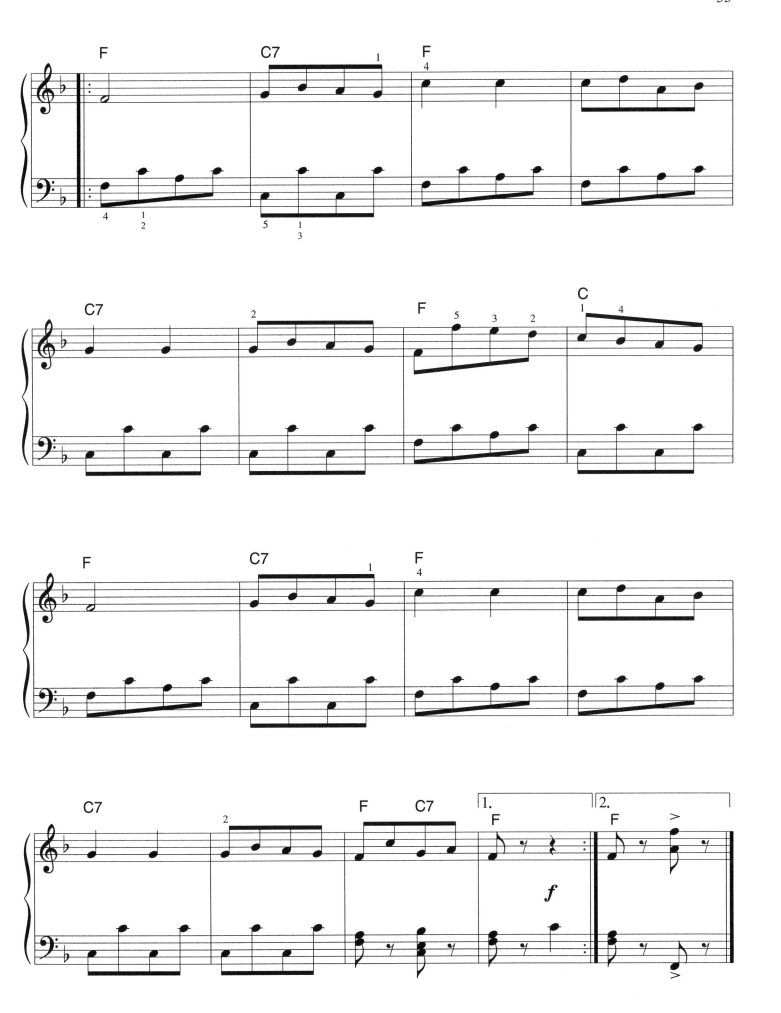

FLIGHT OF THE BUMBLE BEE
(Main theme)

Nicolai Rimsky-Korsakoff

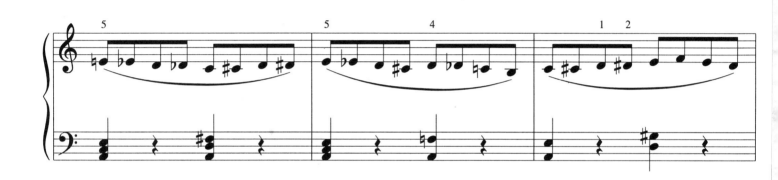

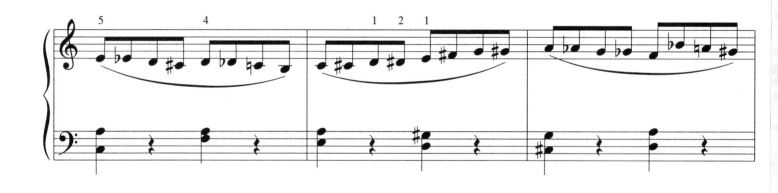

© 1996 Creative Concepts Publishing Corporation
All Rights Reserved

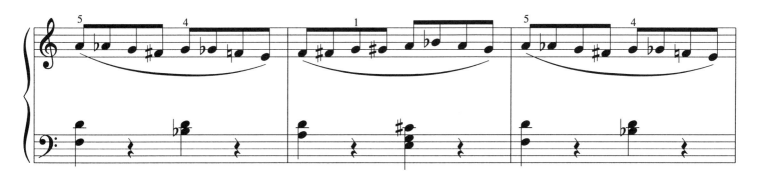

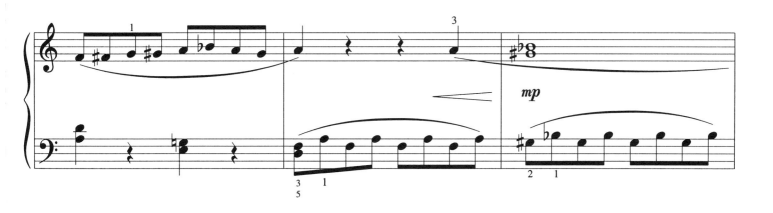

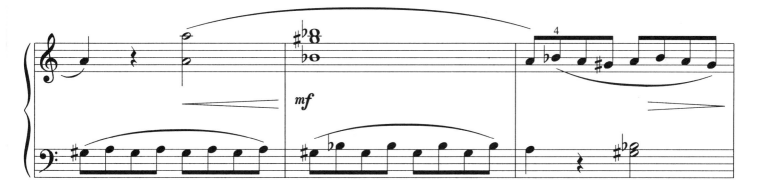

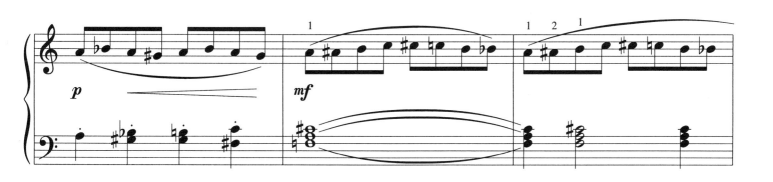

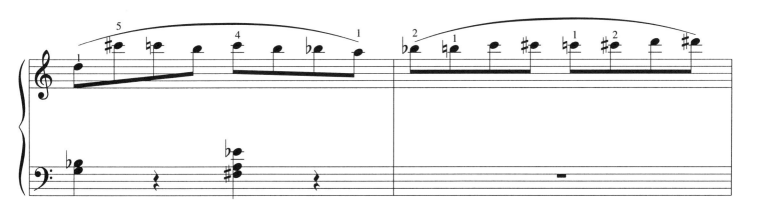

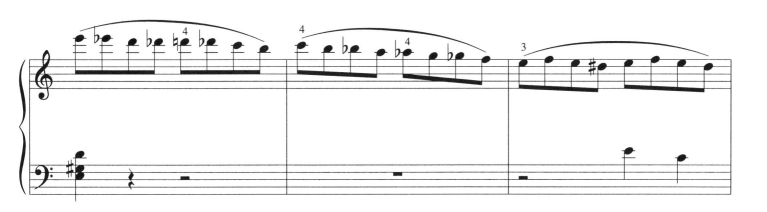

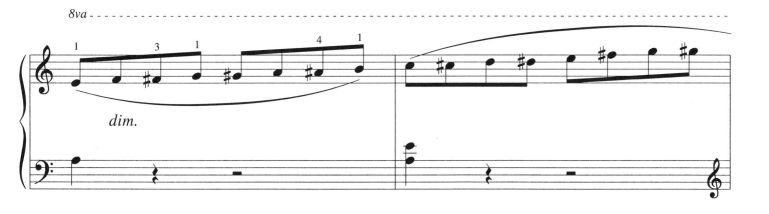

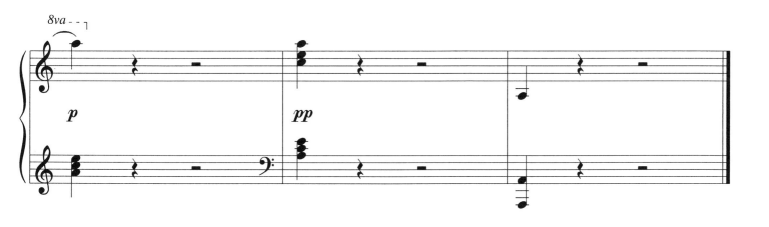

HALLELUJAH CHORUS

(from "The Messiah")

George Frederic Handel

© 1996 Creative Concepts Publishing Corporation
All Rights Reserved

HUNGARIAN DANCE NO. 5

Allegro

Johannes Brahms

© 1996 Creative Concepts Publishing Corporation
All Rights Reserved

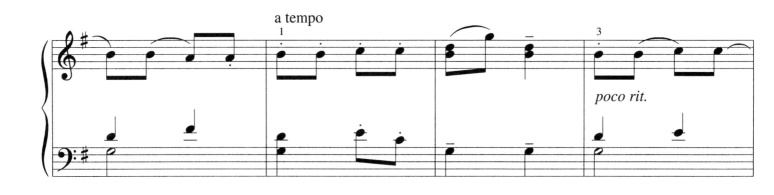

D.C. al Fine

IN THE HALL OF THE MOUNTAIN KING

(from "Peer Gynt")

Edvard Grieg

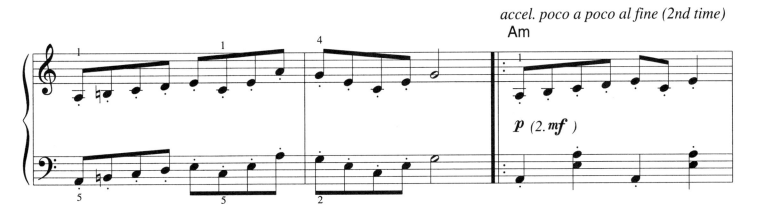

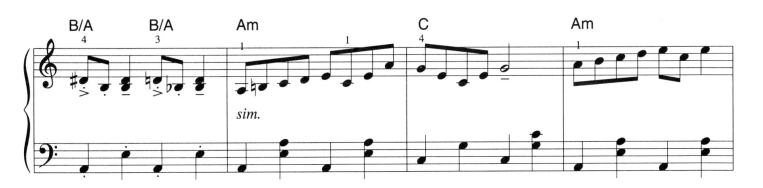

© 1996 Creative Concepts Publishing Corporation
All Rights Reserved

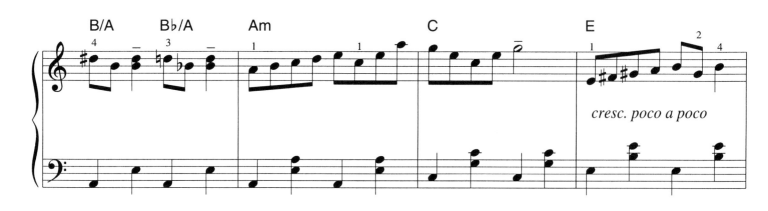

LARGO
(From "New World Symphony")

Anton Dvorak

© 1996 Creative Concepts Publishing Corporation
All Rights Reserved

LITTLE FAIRY WALTZ

Louis Streabbog

Valse moderato

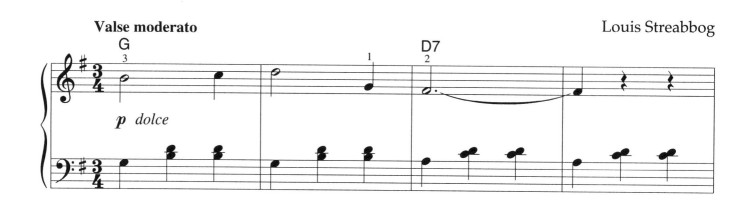

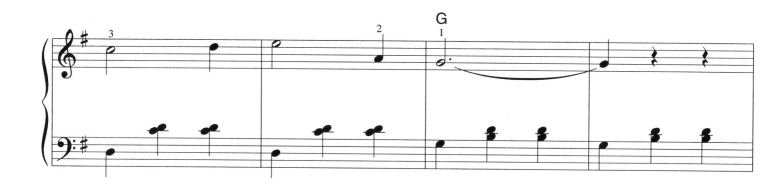

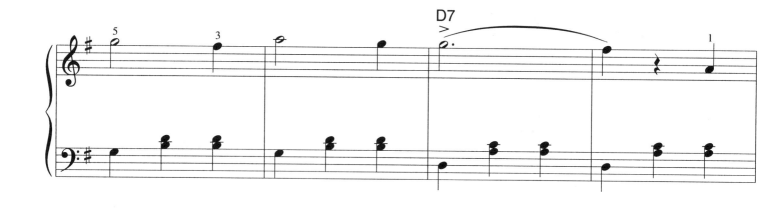

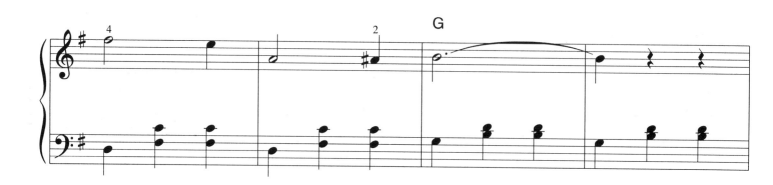

© 1996 Creative Concepts Publishing Corporation
All Rights Reserved

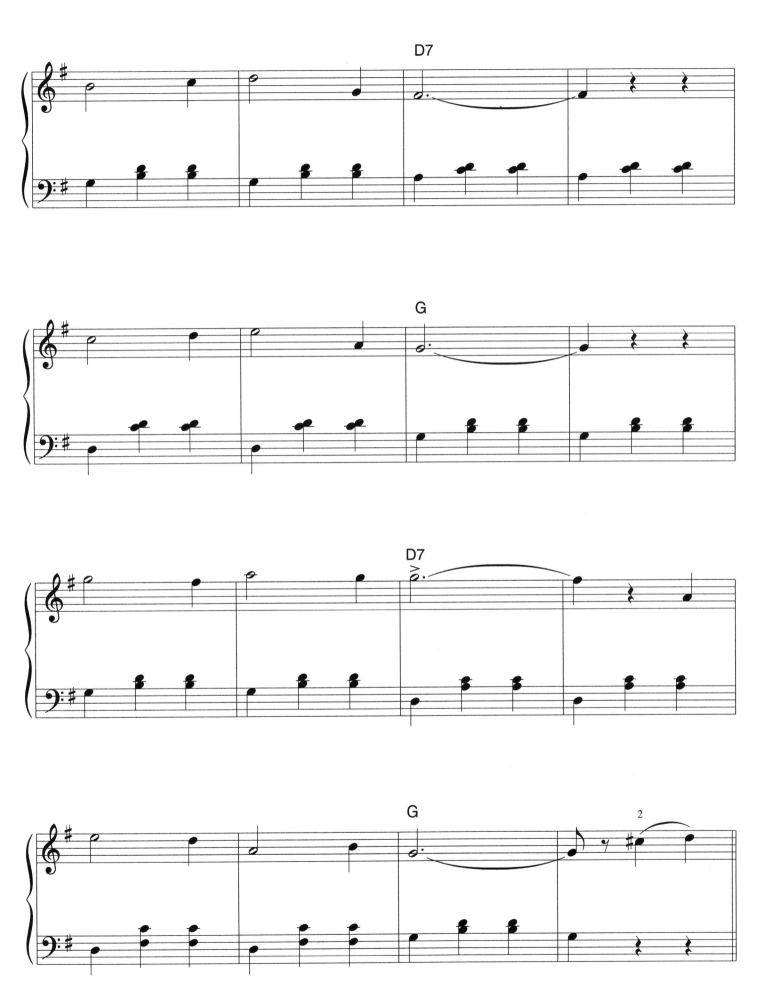

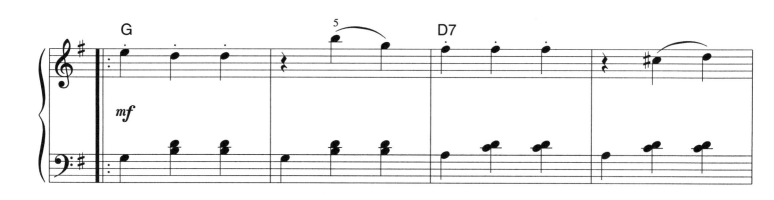

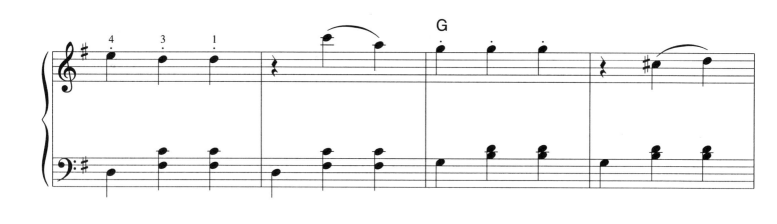

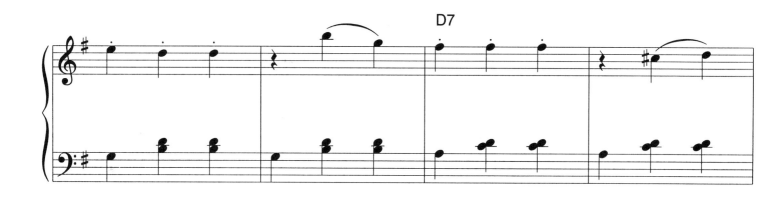

MINUET
(FROM SONATA IN E♭)

Wolfgang Amadeus Mozart

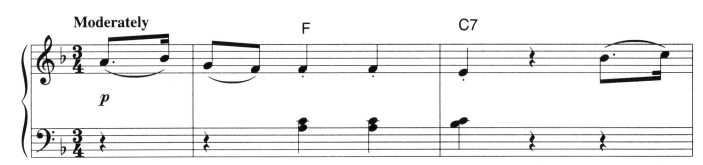

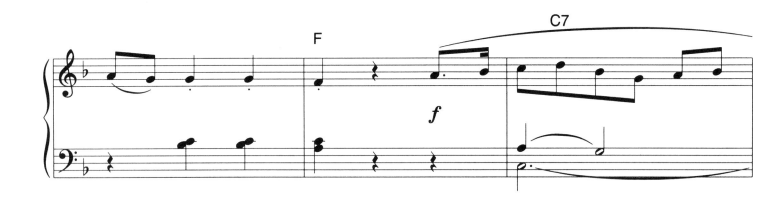

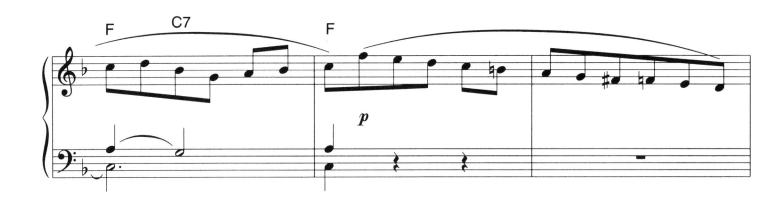

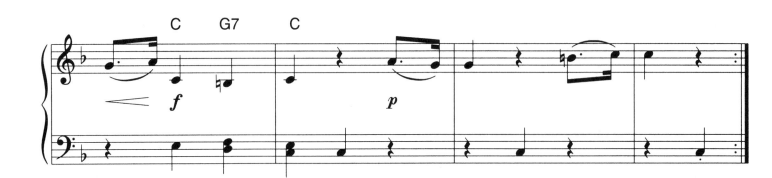

© 1996 Creative Concepts Publishing Corporation
All Rights Reserved

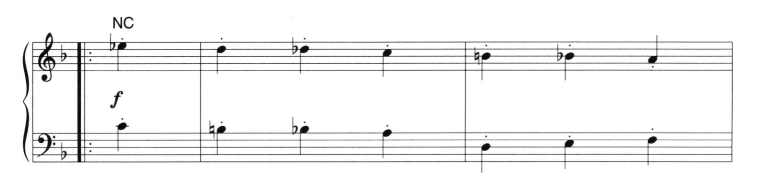

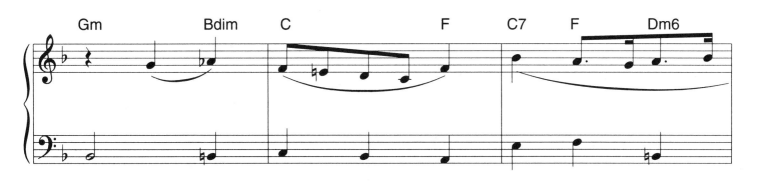

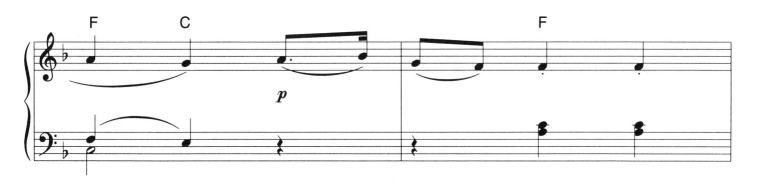

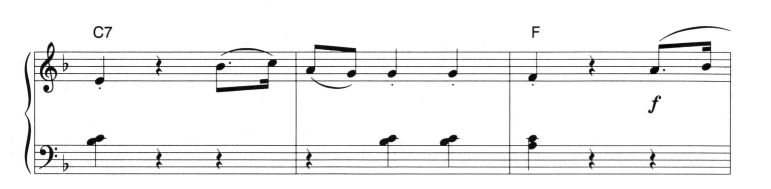

ONE FINE DAY
(from "Madam Butterfly")

Giacomo Puccini

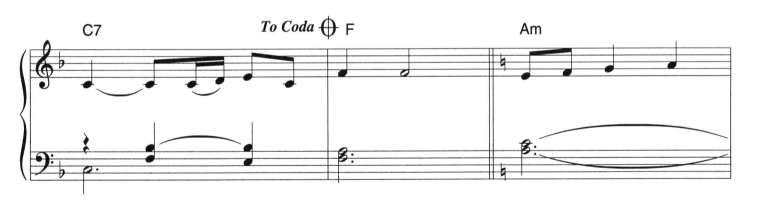

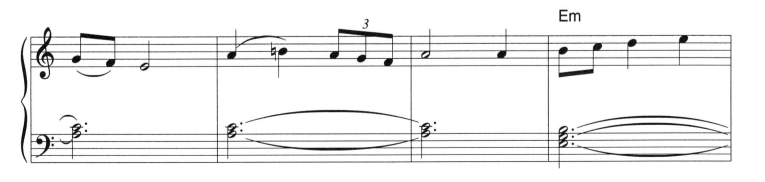

© 1996 Creative Concepts Publishing Corporation
All Rights Reserved

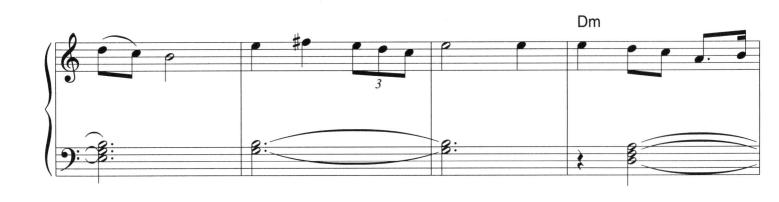

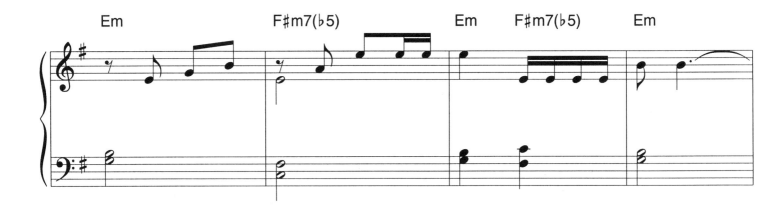

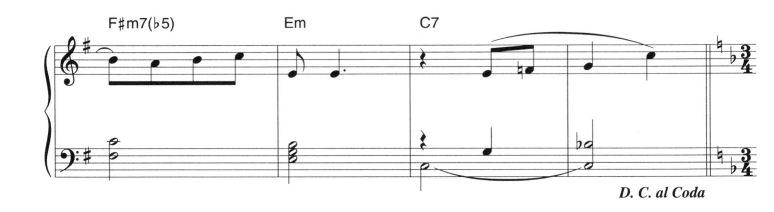

D. C. al Coda

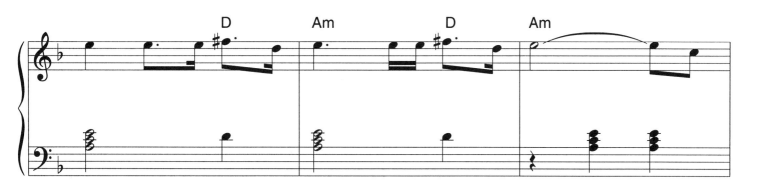

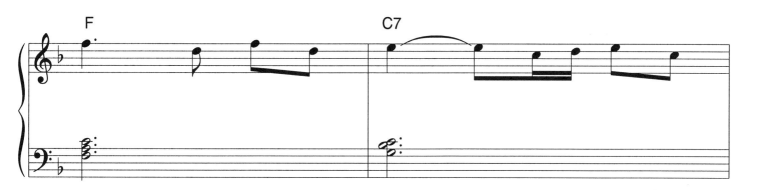

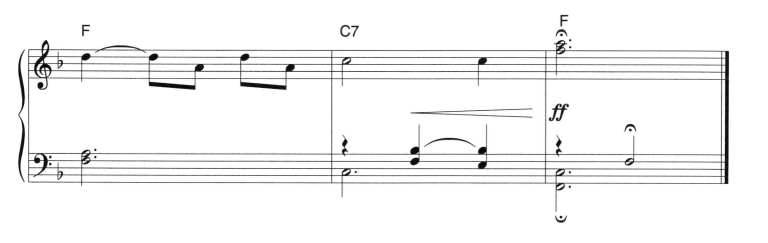

MY HEART AT THY SWEET VOICE
(from "Samson and Delilah")

Camille Saint-Saëns

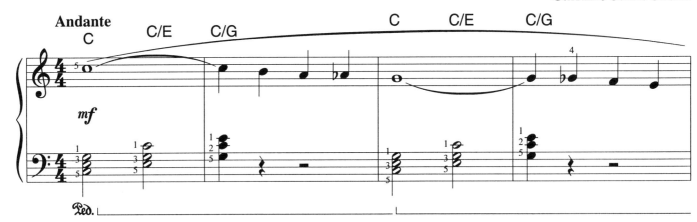

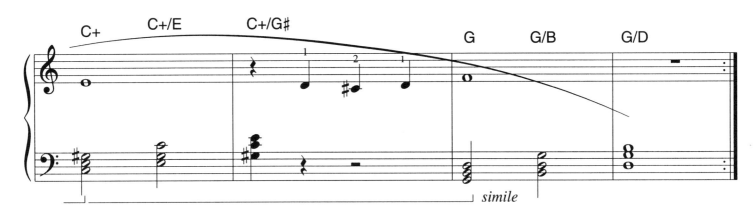

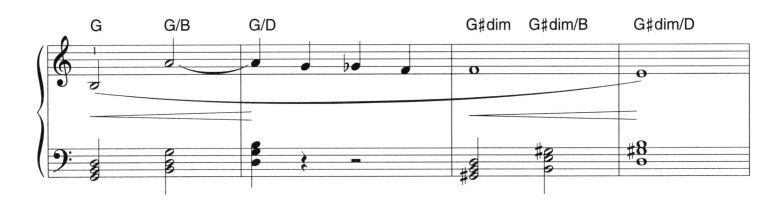

© 1996 Creative Concepts Publishing Corporation
All Rights Reserved

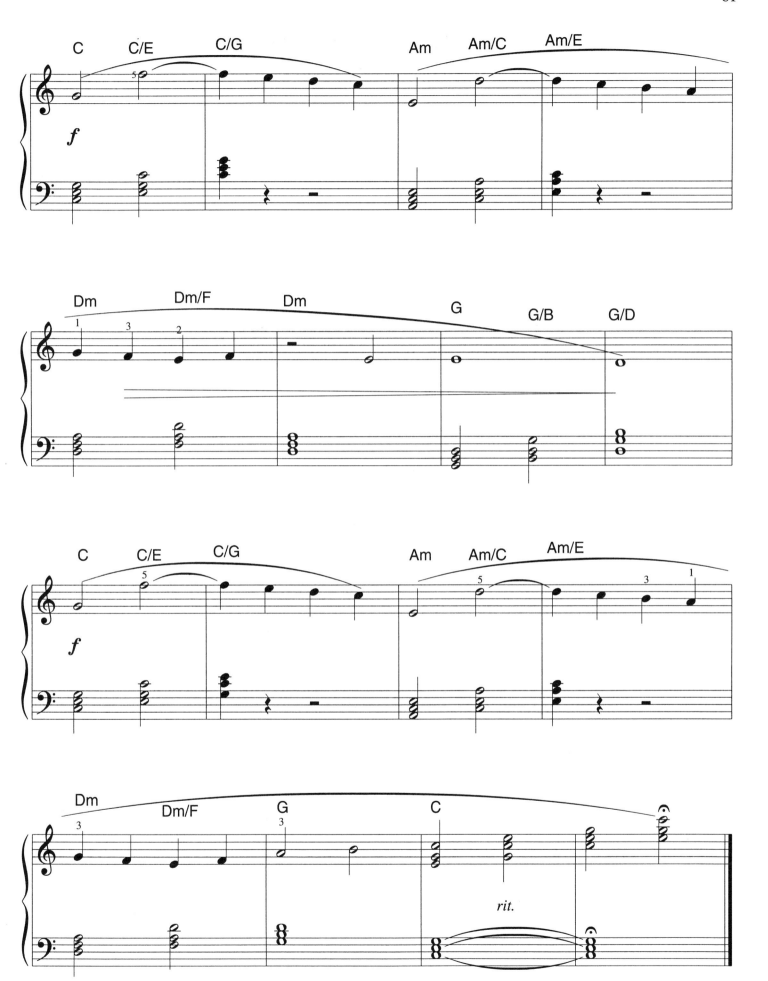

Theme from
PIANO CONCERTO NO. 2

Sergei Rachmaninoff

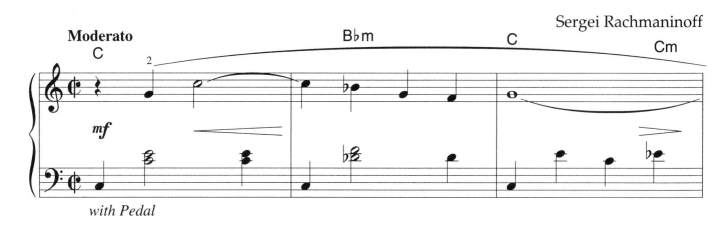

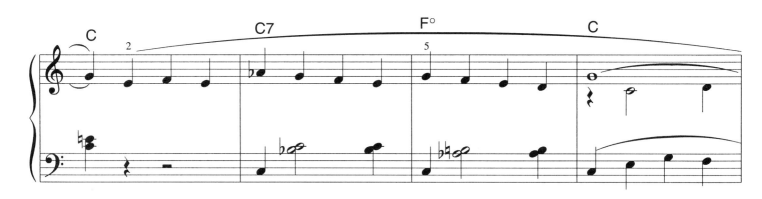

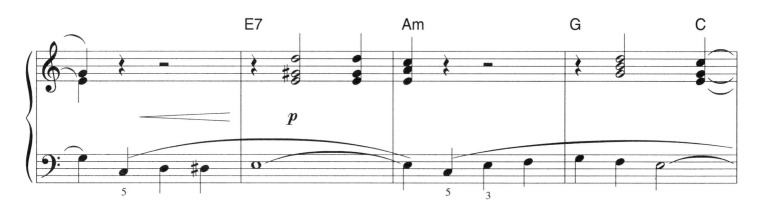

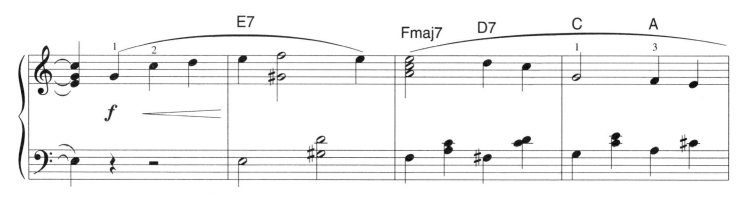

© 1996 Creative Concepts Publishing Corporation
All Rights Reserved

CONCERTO IN E MAJOR, "SPRING"

(from "The Four Seasons")

Antonio Vivaldi

Copyright © 1992 by HAL LEONARD CORPORATION
International Copyright Secured   All Rights Reserved

THEME FROM
PIANO CONCERTO IN C MAJOR
(ELVIRA MADIGAN)

Wolfgang Amadeus Mozart

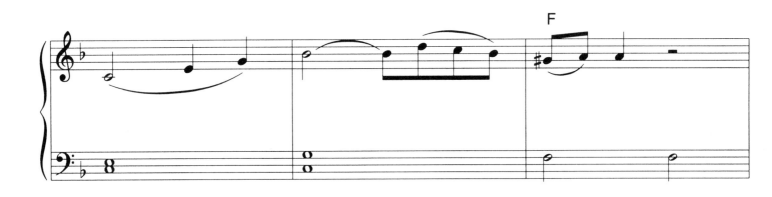

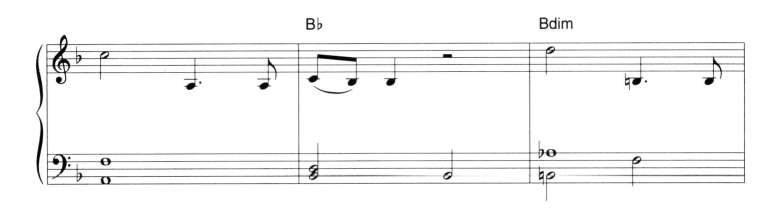

© 1996 Creative Concepts Publishing Corporation
All Rights Reserved

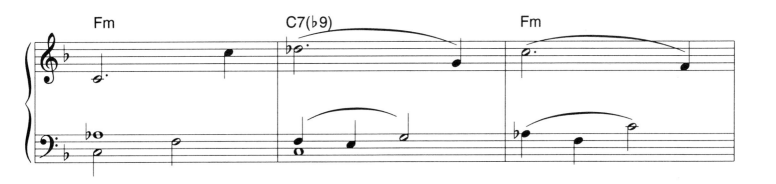

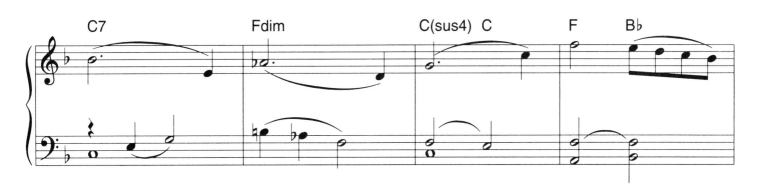

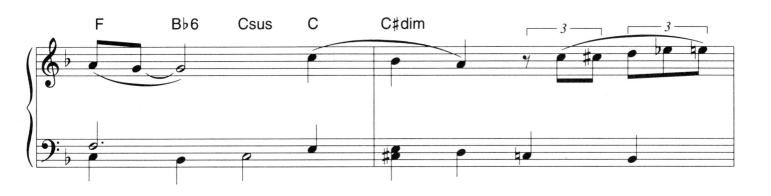

Themes from
PIANO CONCERTO NO. 3
(in C minor)

Ludwig van Beethoven

Moderately fast

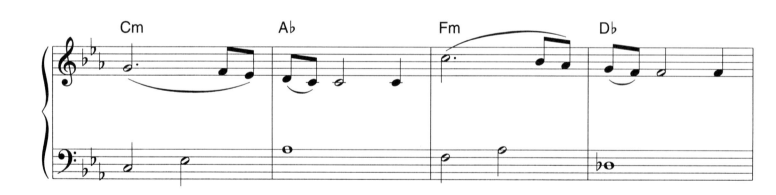

© 1996 Creative Concepts Publishing Corporation
All Rights Reserved

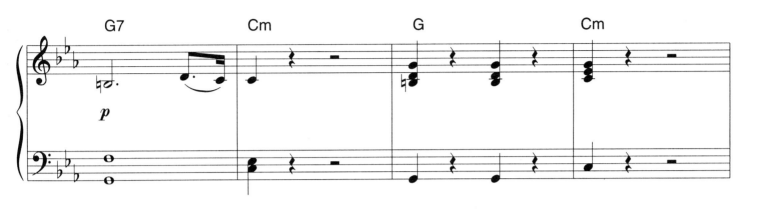

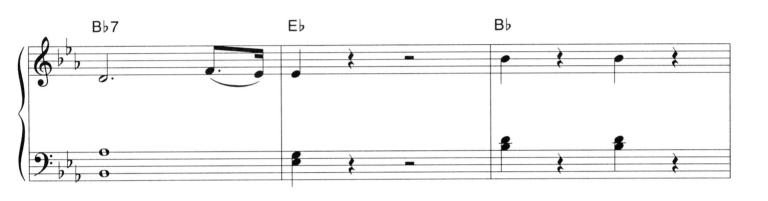

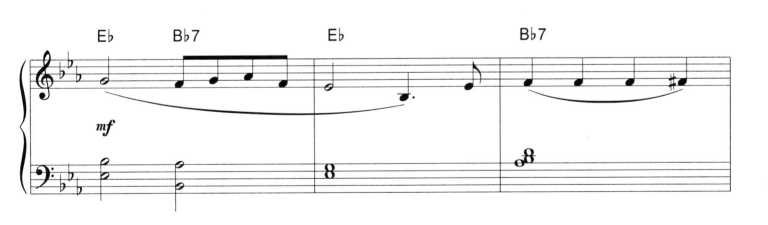

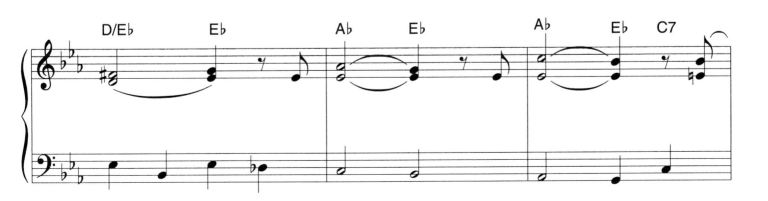

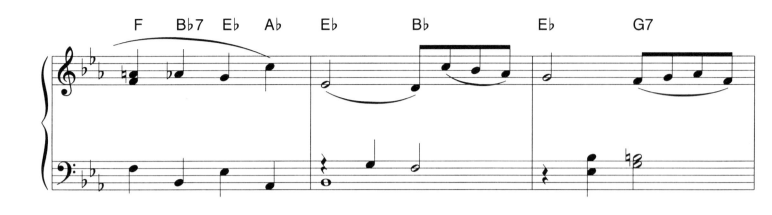

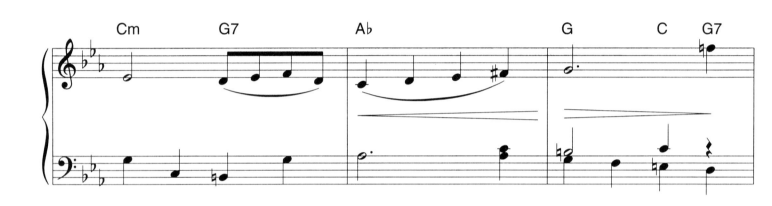

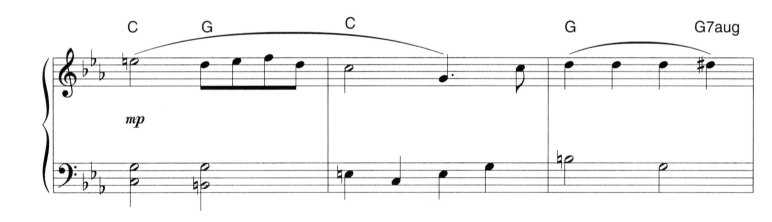

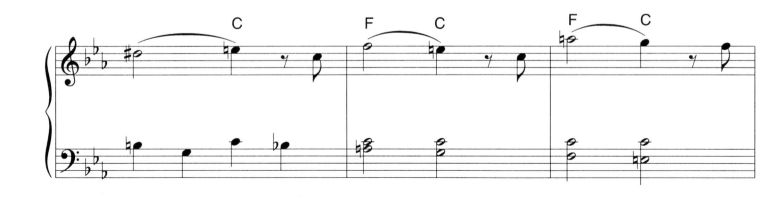

Theme from
PIANO SONATA NO. 2

Ludwig van Beethoven

© 1996 Creative Concepts Publishing Corporation
All Rights Reserved

PRELUDE IN C
(from "The Well-Tempered Clavier" Vol. 1)

Johann Sebastian Bach

Smoothly

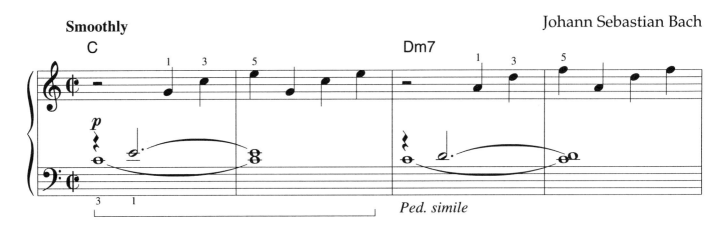

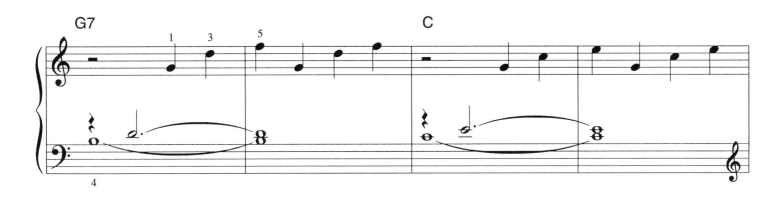

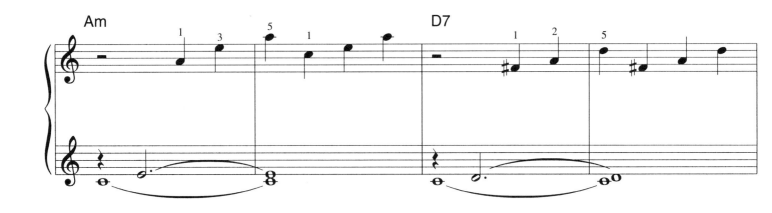

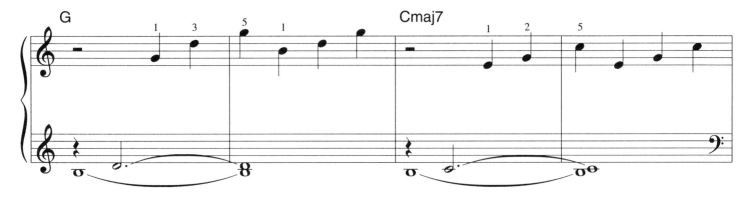

© 1996 Creative Concepts Publishing Corporation
All Rights Reserved

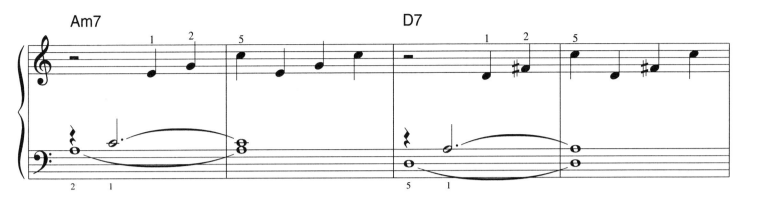

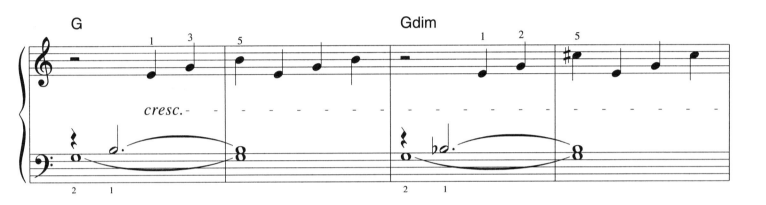

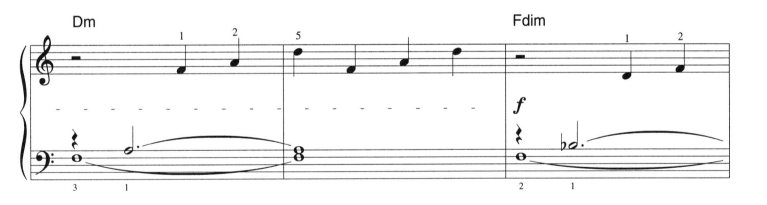

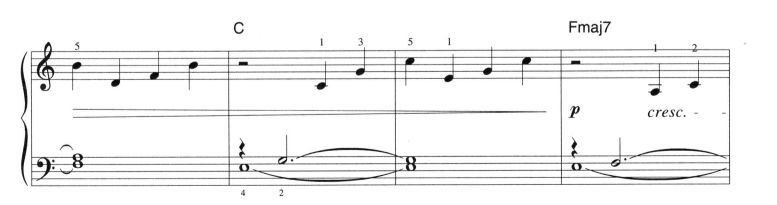

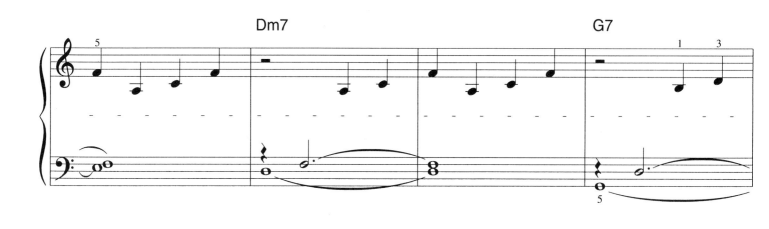

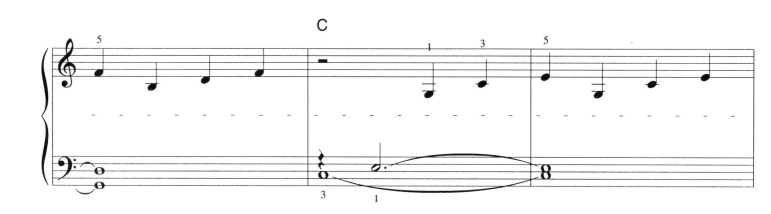

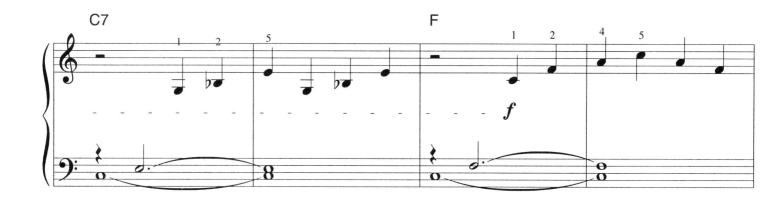

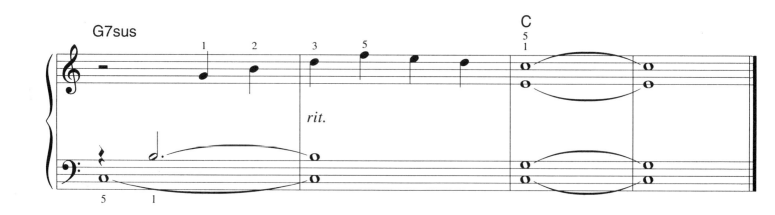

LULLABY

Johannes Brahms

© 1984 by HAL LEONARD CORPORATION
International Copyright Secured   All Rights Reserved

ROMANCE

Anton Rubinstein

© 1996 Creative Concepts Publishing Corporation
All Rights Reserved

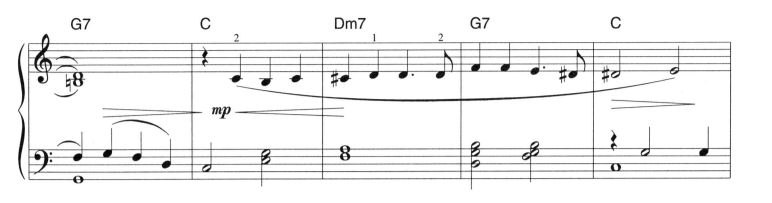

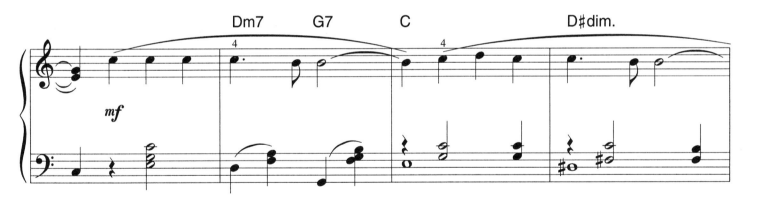

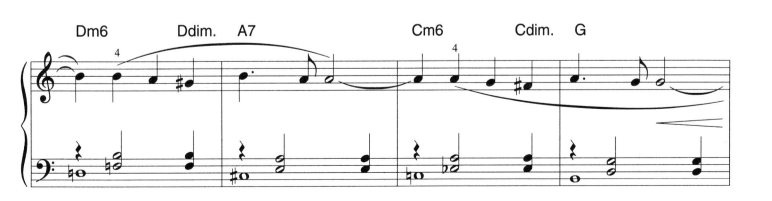

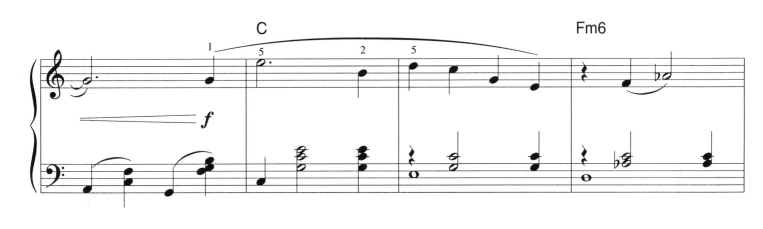

SALUT D'AMOUR

Edward Elgar

© 1996 Creative Concepts Publishing Corporation
All Rights Reserved

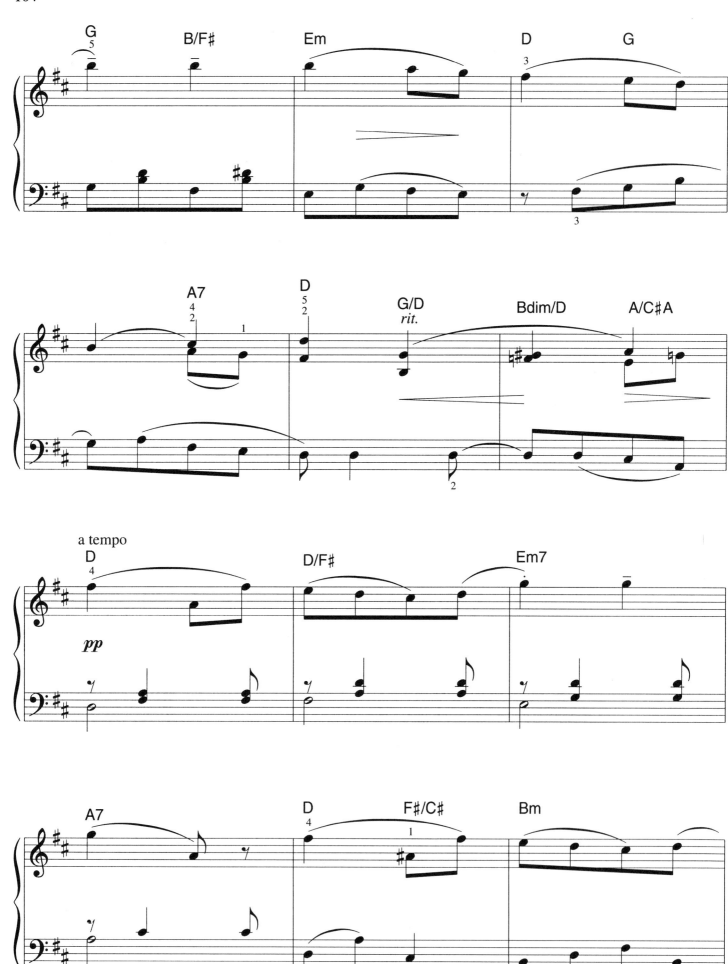

SCHERZO
(from Symphony No. 2 in D)

Ludwig van Beethoven

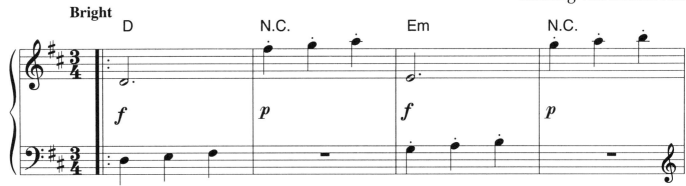

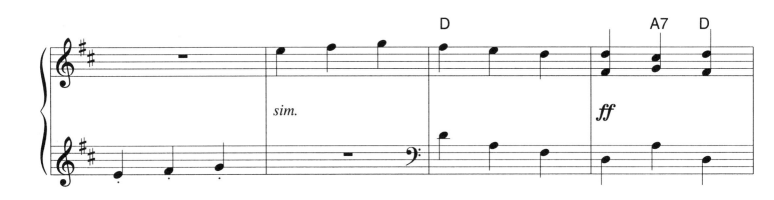

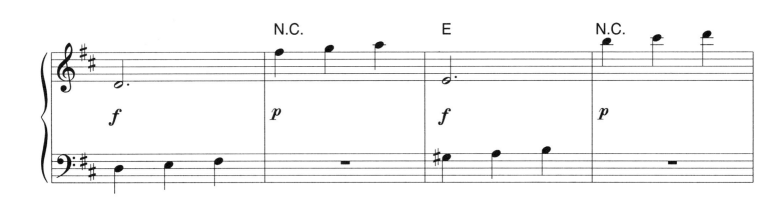

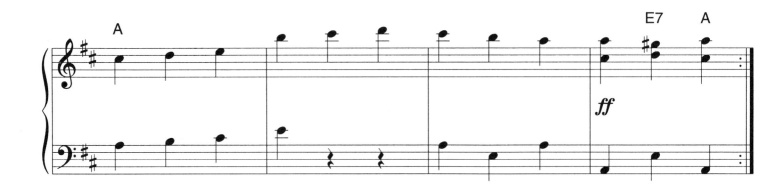

© 1996 Creative Concepts Publishing Corporation
All Rights Reserved

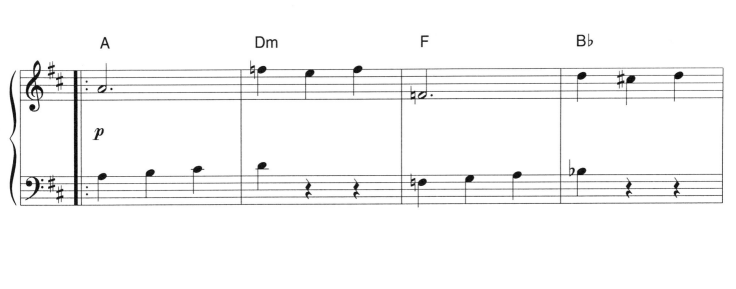

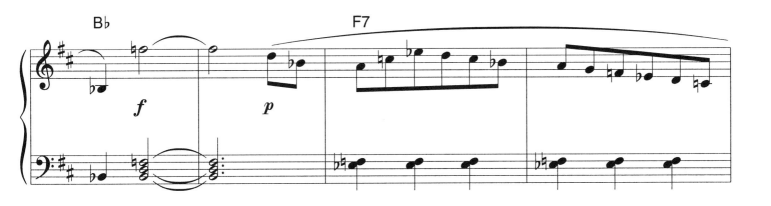

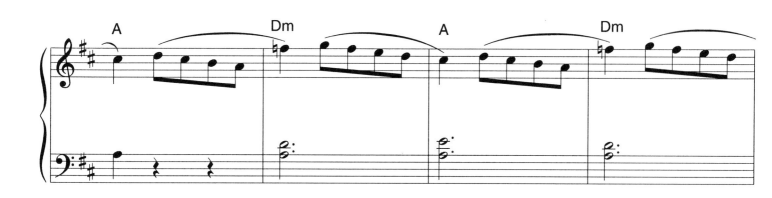

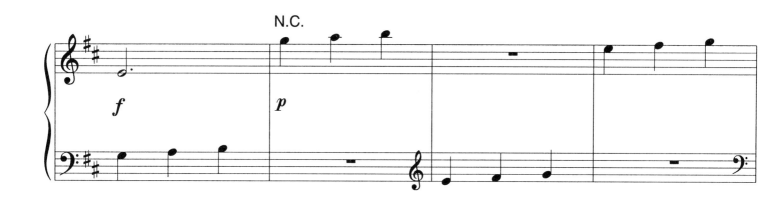

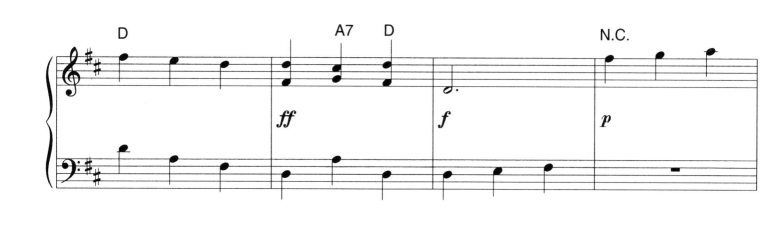

110

SOLDIERS' CHORUS
(From "Faust")

Charles Gounod

© 1996 Creative Concepts Publishing Corporation
All Rights Reserved

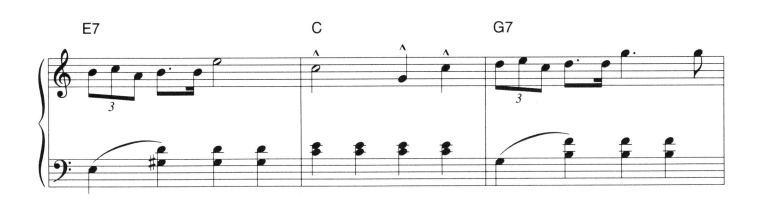

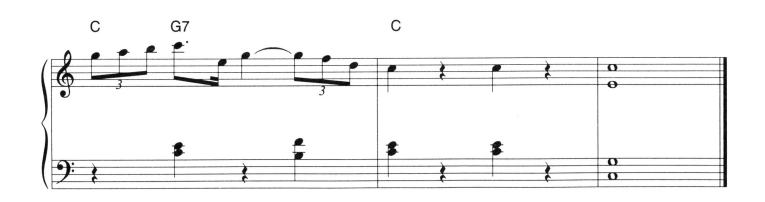

SONG OF INDIA

Nikolai Rimsky-Korsakov

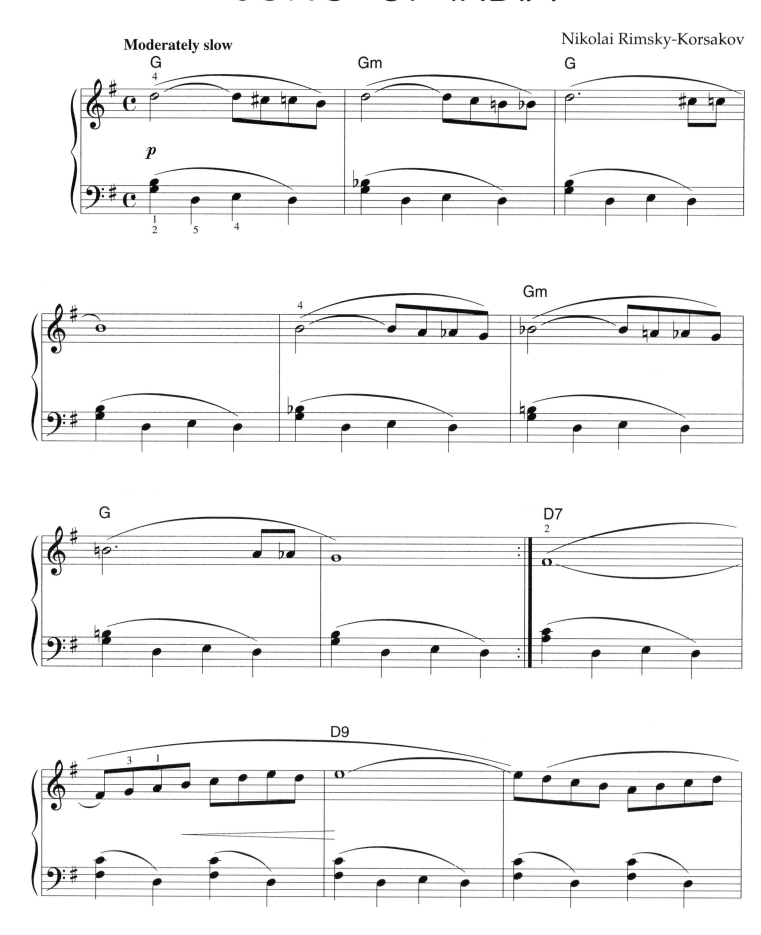

© 1996 Creative Concepts Publishing Corporation
All Rights Reserved

SPINNING SONG

Albert Ellmenreich

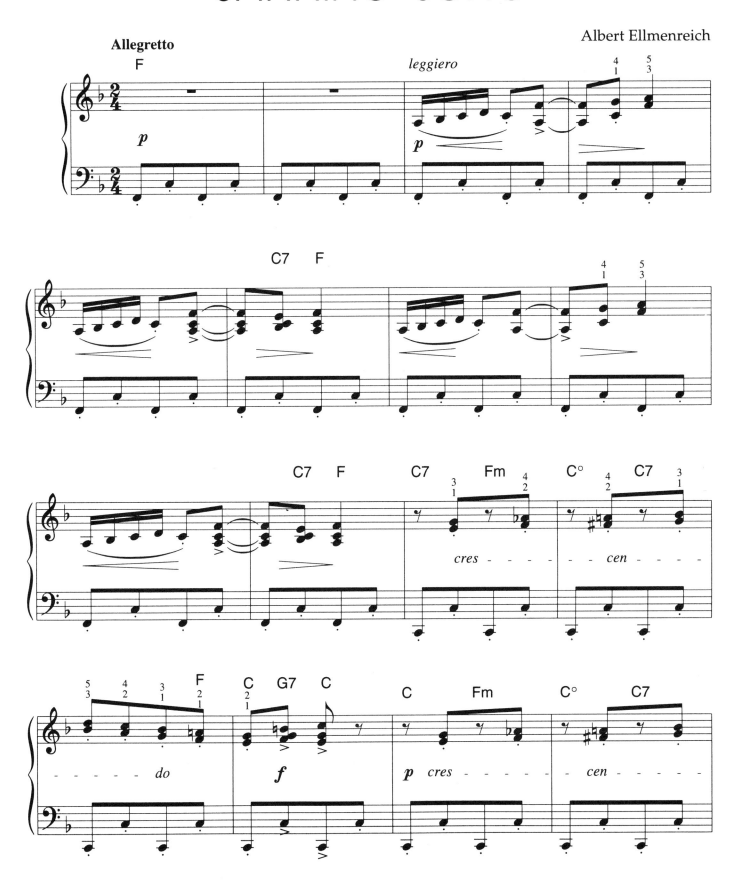

© 1996 Creative Concepts Publishing Corporation
All Rights Reserved

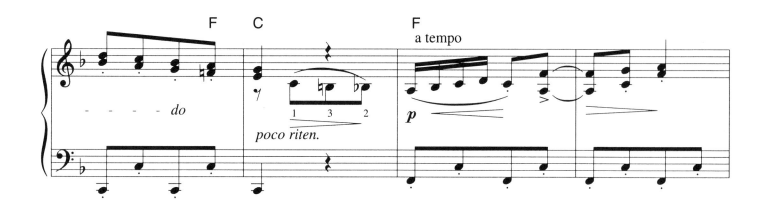

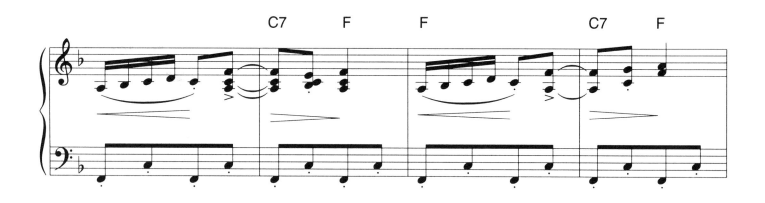

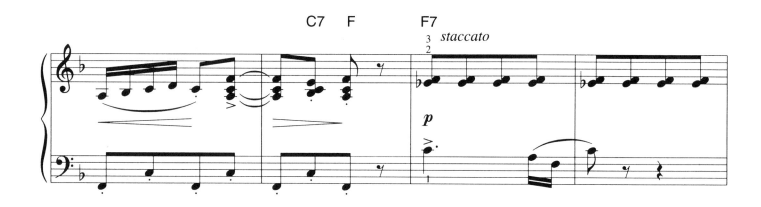

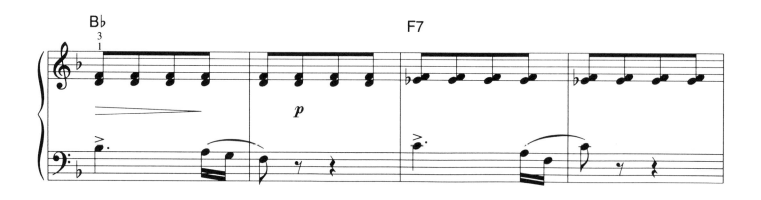

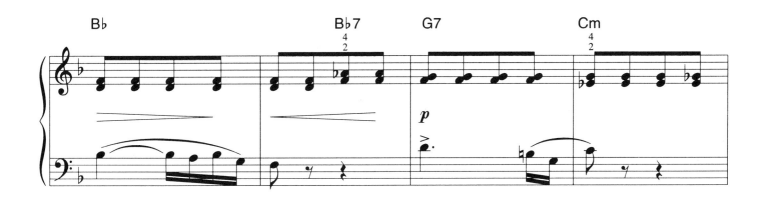

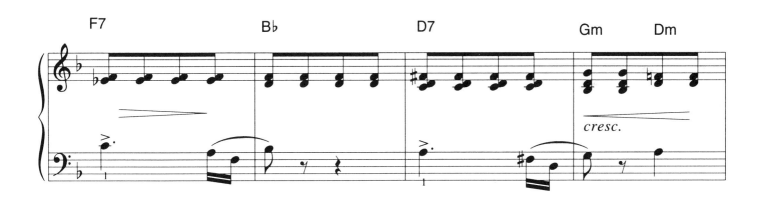

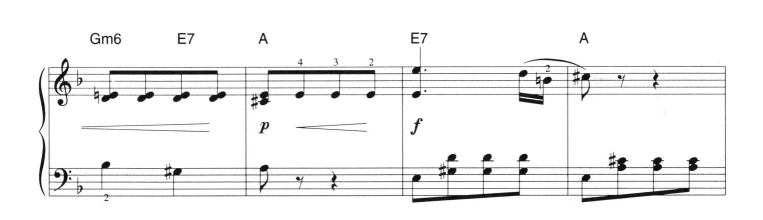

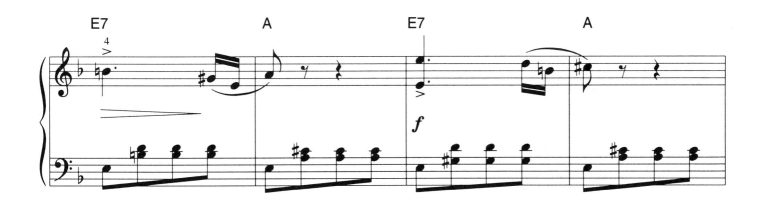

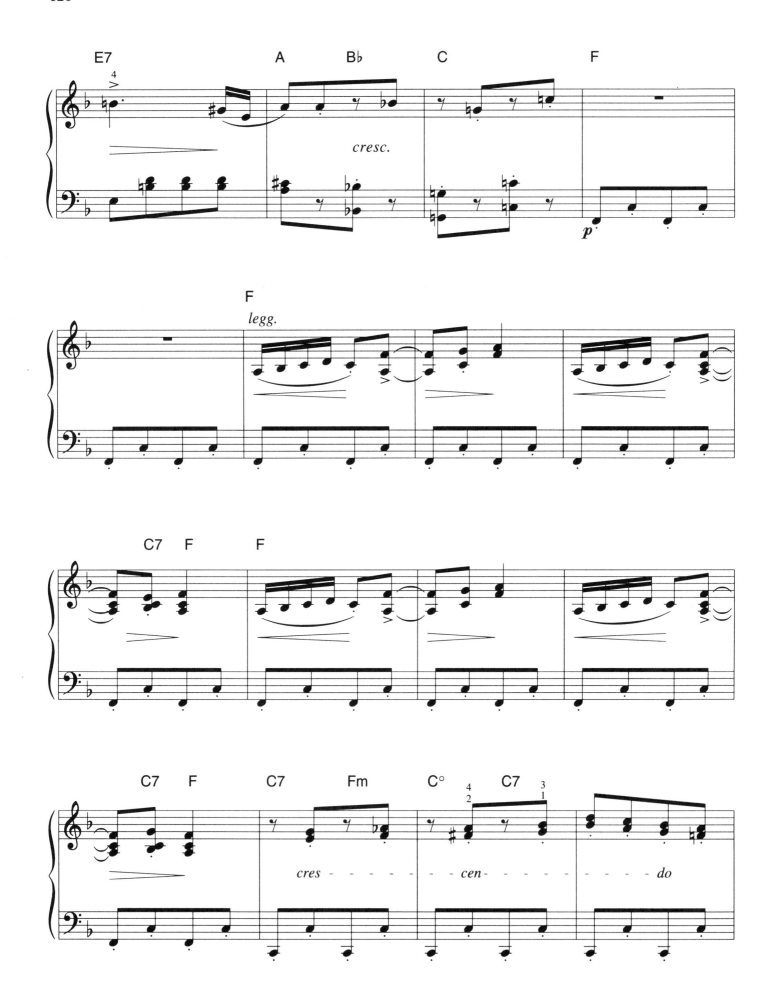

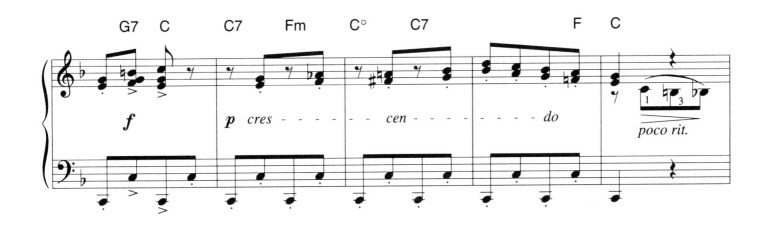

THE SORCERER'S APPRENTICE

Paul Dukas

© 1996 Creative Concepts Publishing Corporation
All Rights Reserved

TOCCATA IN D MINOR

Johann Sebastian Bach

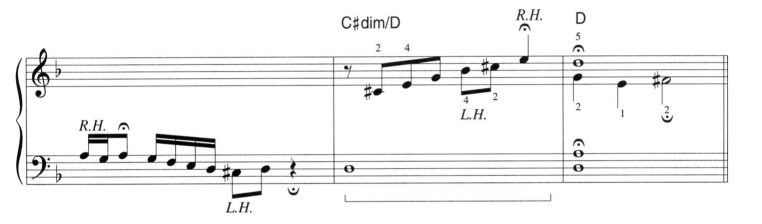

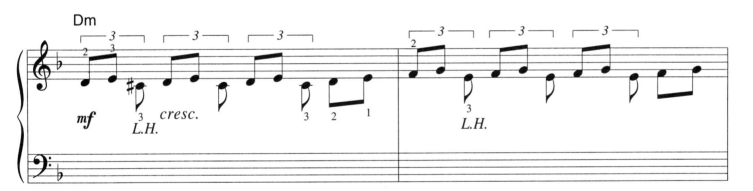

© 1996 Creative Concepts Publishing Corporation
All Rights Reserved

126

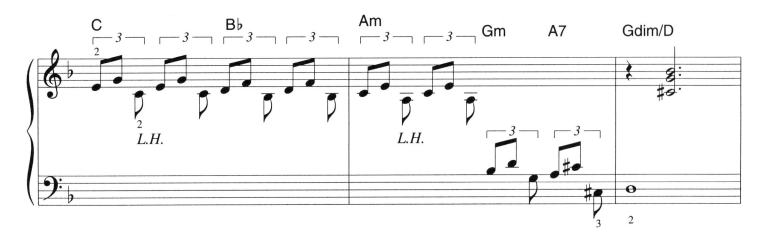

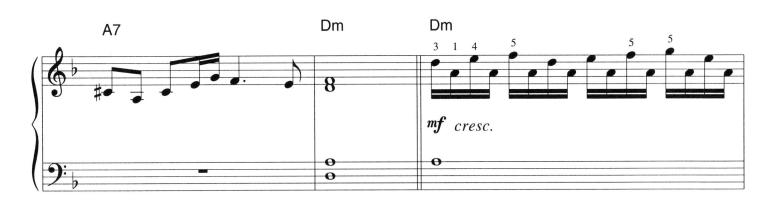

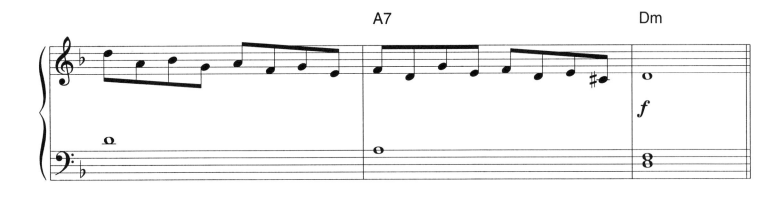

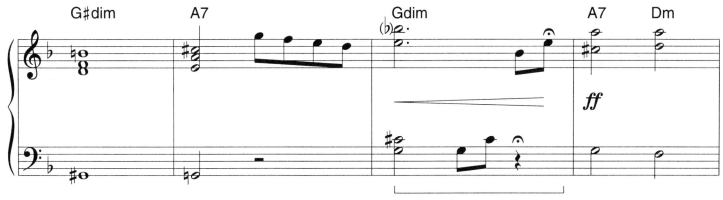

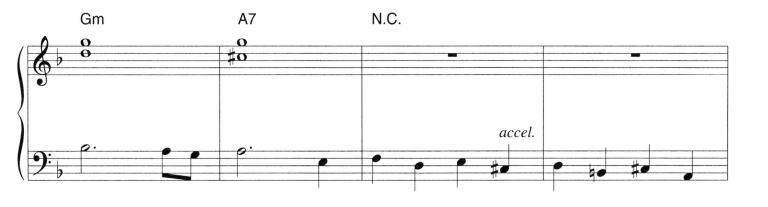

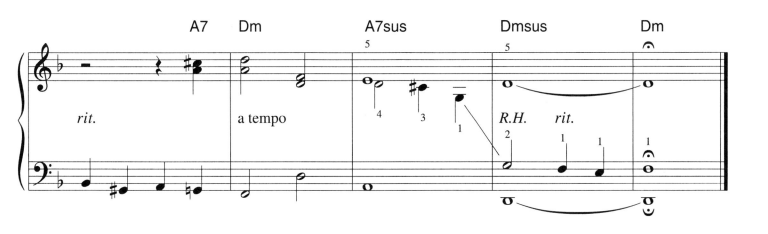

Theme from
SYMPHONY NO. 1

Johannes Brahms

Allegro non troppo

mp

cresc.

© 1996 Creative Concepts Publishing Corporation
All Rights Reserved

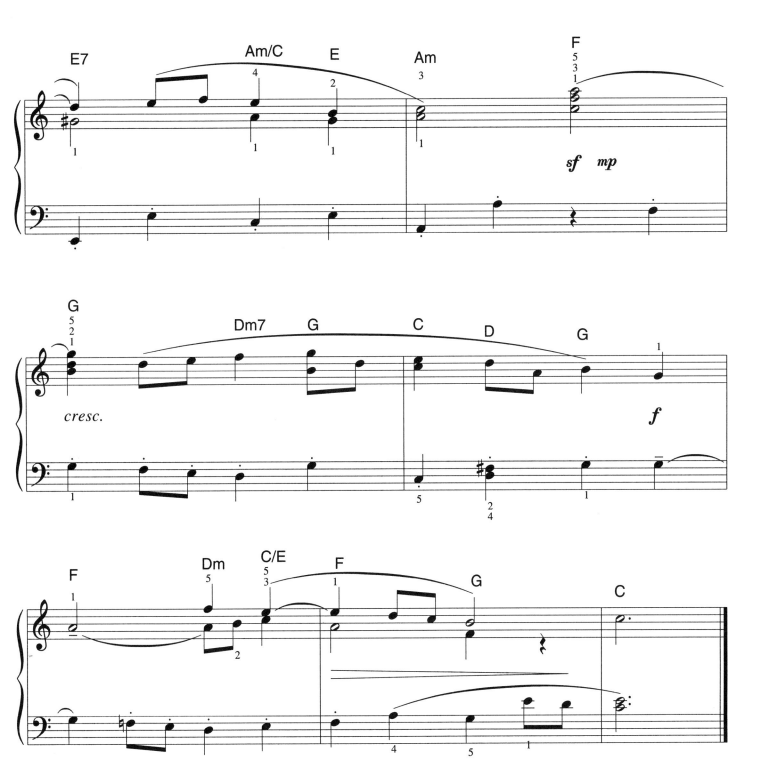

Theme from
SYMPHONY NO. 5

Ludwig van Beethoven

© 1996 Creative Concepts Publishing Corporation
All Rights Reserved

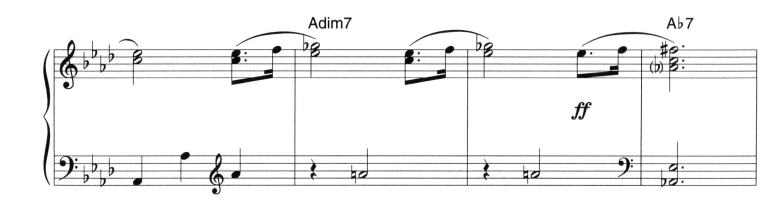

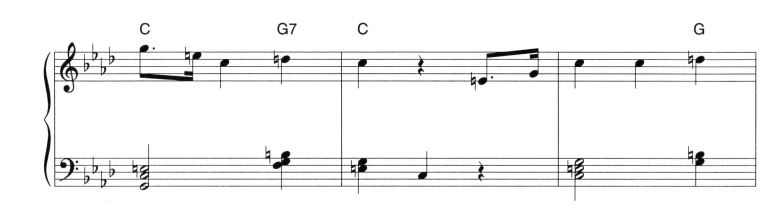

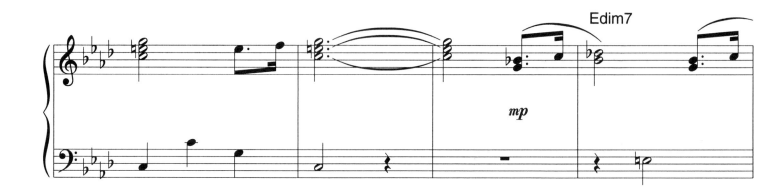

VIOLIN CONCERTO
(Theme from the 3rd Movement)

Ludwig van Beethoven

Allegro

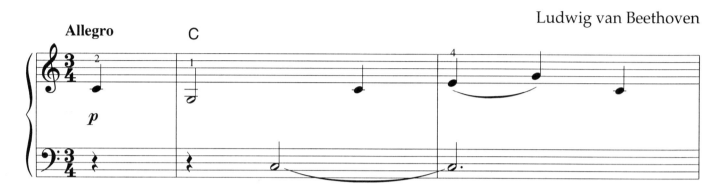

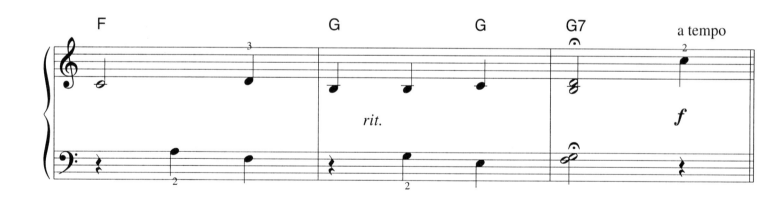

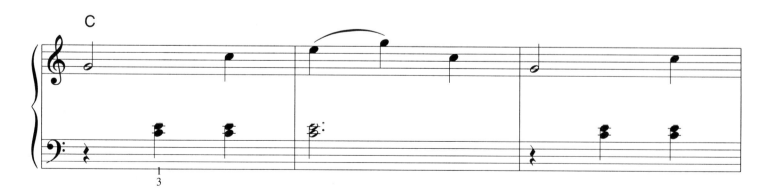

© 1996 Creative Concepts Publishing Corporation
All Rights Reserved

WALTZ
(from "The Sleeping Beauty")

Pyotr Ilyich Tchaikovsky

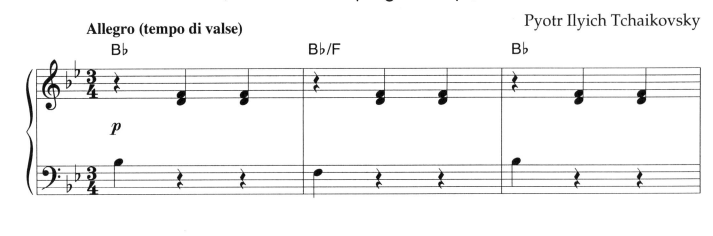

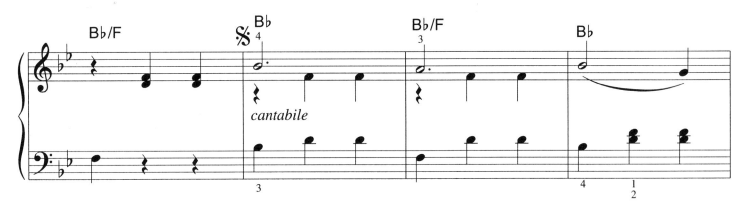

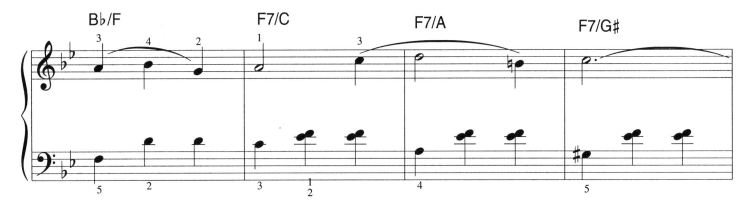

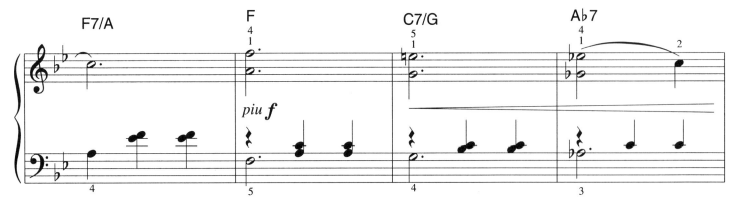

© 1996 Creative Concepts Publishing Corporation
All Rights Reserved

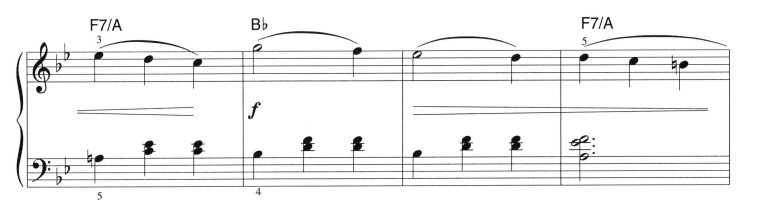

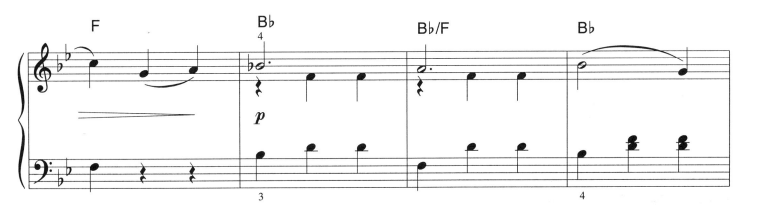

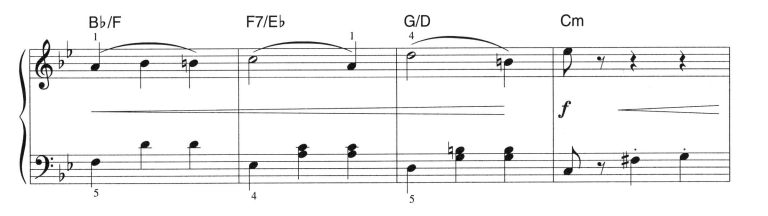

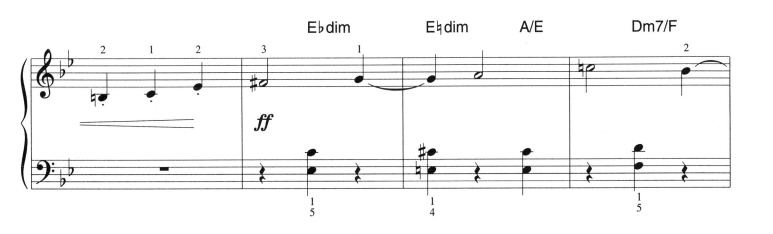

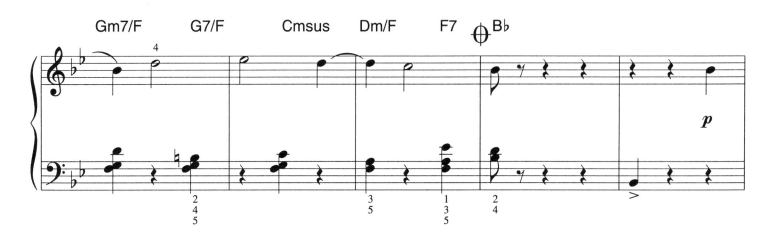

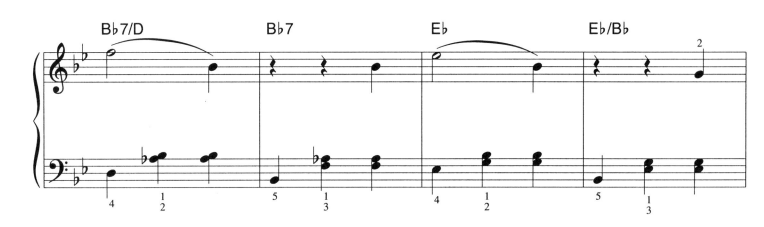

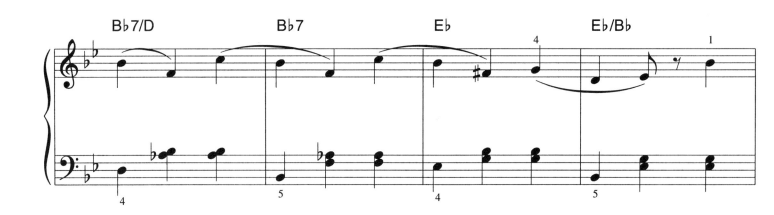

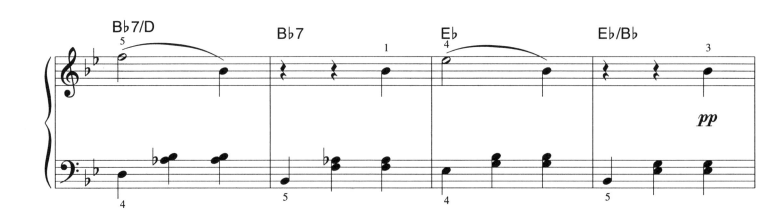

WOODPECKER WALTZ
(Opus 63)

Louis Streabbog

Valse moderato con moto

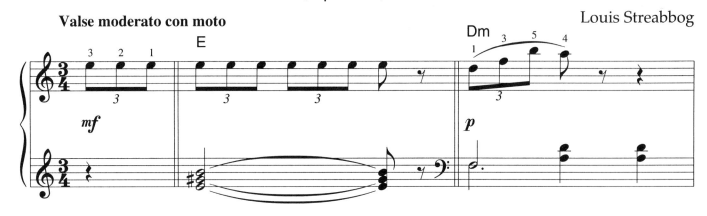

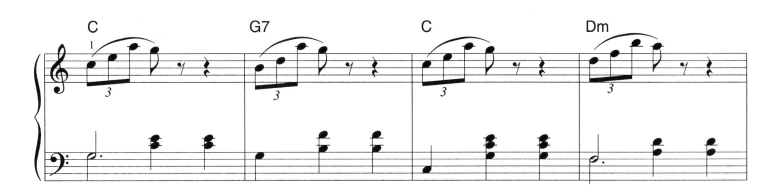

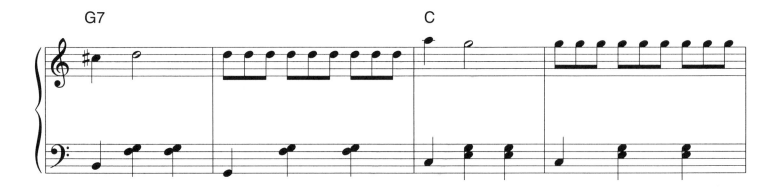

© 1996 Creative Concepts Publishing Corporation
All Rights Reserved

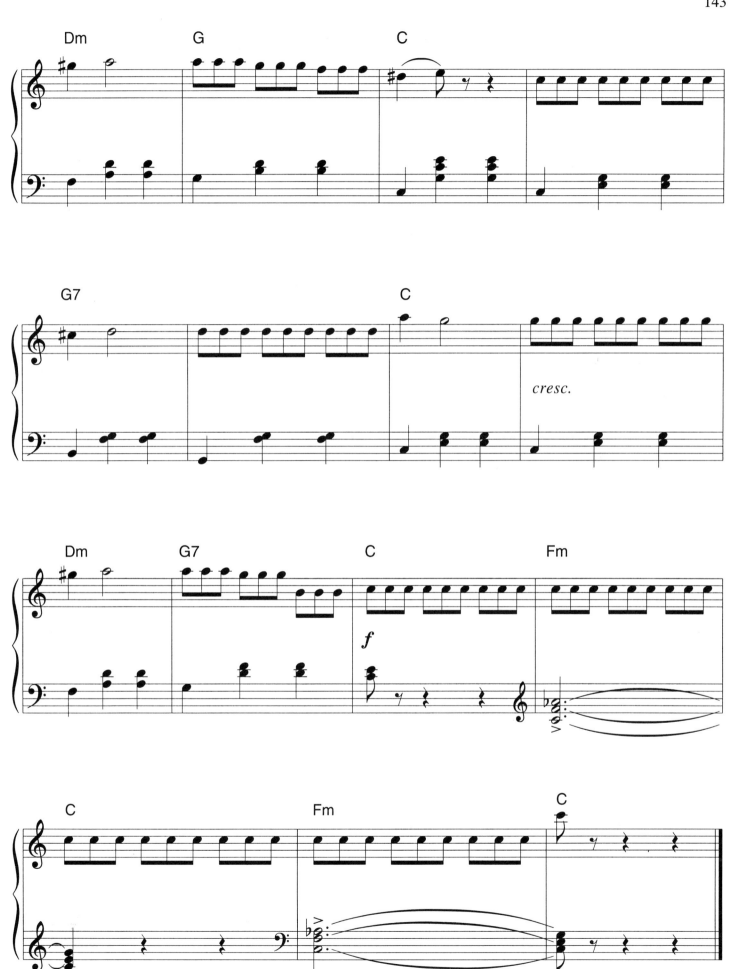

TRUMPET TUNE

Henry Purcell

© 1996 Creative Concepts Publishing Corporation
All Rights Reserved